Etched *in* Stone

Etched
in Stone

A Study of
Biblical Personalities

By
**Rabbi Dr.
Walter Orenstein**

published by Bash Publications, Inc. New York

ETCHED IN STONE

FIRST EDITION
First Impression — MAY 1989

Published by
bp Inc.
705 Foster Avenue
Brooklyn, New York 11230

(718) 692-3900

ISBN 0—932351—24—7

Typography by **bp** Inc.
Printed in the U.S.A.

to my grandchildren עמו״ש
Aviva and Shoshana Cytryn
and
Natan David Drucker

Table of Contents

Preface

This book is the result of many years of teaching Torah to eager and astute college students at the Teachers Institute for Women (TIW) and to serious-minded adults in synagogues and community centers, all of whom were deeply concerned and involved with the message of the Torah for contemporary man. The material has been culled from a variety of traditional Jewish sources — Talmud, Midrash, Bible commentary, and articles and lectures by contemporary theologians. All sources have been carefully annotated, in order to afford those who may wish to study the material further the opportunity to do so. While the work is primarily addressed to the yeshiva student and layman — who are strongly advised to familiarize themselves with the appropriate Biblical texts — the scholar will also find the work worthwhile for its novel approach and its choice and organization of material.

With regard to the rendering of Scriptural passages, the "new translation" of the Bible by the Jewish Publication Society has been used almost exclusively. Its simple and free-flowing style lends itself to easier reading and better comprehension.

When a commentator is quoted for the first time, he is identified by full name, date, and country of origin, to put his work into perspective.

Since the primary purpose of this work is to delineate the lives of Biblical personalities, thus bringing into focus their unique contributions, some narratives are discussed in detail while others are mentioned briefly, depending upon the relevance of such material to the issue at hand.

I wish to express sincerest appreciation to my students, past and present, who encouraged this endeavor by their interest in my lectures, their questions, and their own thoughts on the material. I shall forever remain indebted to them for having touched my life.

Lastly, let it be noted that this work would never have reached fruition were it not for the patience and perseverance of my wife Nellie, who carefully read the manuscript and offered many creative suggestions for improvement of style and clarity of expression. She is, indeed, the personification of the words of King Solomon: "Her husband trusts in her and he never lacks gain."

Part I

The Patriarchs
And Matriarchs

Introduction

Said R. Yizhak: The Torah should have commenced with "This month shall be unto you the first of months," which is the first command given to Israel. What is the reason, then, that it commences with the account of the creation? Because of (the thought expressed in the text) "He declared to the people the power of His works in order that He might give them the heritage of the nations" (Psalms 111:6).

(Rashi: Bereshit 1)

It is important that we understand what prompted Rabbi Shlomo, son of Yizhak (Rashi), the renowned Bible commentator of 11th century France, to begin his commentary with this question. On the surface, the question seems rather naive. The first chapter of Bereshit establishes that the Almighty is the creator of the world — its Master. All things that exist in the world are responsible to Him, and man is no exception. It is therefore fitting that a code of law, given by the Almighty to man, be introduced with a narrative establishing these truths. As such, Rashi's question is most perplexing.

This point is made by Rabbi Moshe, son of Nahman (Ramban), the 13th century Spanish Bible commentator par excellence who is also known as Nahmanides. Nevertheless, says Ramban, when seen from another perspective, the question is most logical. For "The process of creation is a deep mystery not to be understood from the verses and it cannot truly be known, except through the tradition going back to Moses our teacher, who received it from the mouth of the Almighty; and those who know it are obligated to conceal it." As such, it would have been enough for our people to have been told, "For in six days the Lord made heaven and earth, the sea and all that is in them, and rested on the seventh day" (Shemot 20:11).

Why then did the Torah begin with creation?

Rashi postulates that the Torah begins with the story of creation to legitimize the right of the Jewish people to the Promised Land. As Creator of the world, the Almighty may give the land to whomever He chooses, for however long. Ramban adds that the purpose of the whole Torah narrative, from the creation to the settling of the land of Canaan by the Israelites, is to teach humanity that the Almighty created man to reign over all His works. Despite this noble calling, however, man sinned, incurring God's wrath and punishment. If so, says Ramban, it is proper that the sinners lose their land and it be given to another nation. Indeed, such has been God's rule in the world from the beginning. Avraham was the father of such a nation; his seed inherited the land of Canaan.

We shall expand on the words of Rashi and Ramban, and develop the theme somewhat more fully.

Fundamentally, it is quite true that the story of creation appears in the Torah to establish that God created the world. But of far greater importance to the reader, it establishes when, how, and to what end man was created. The narrative material from Adam to Avraham illustrates this and delineates how early man fared in the environment in which he was placed, the challenges he faced, and the choices he made. It is a tale of egocentricity and sin, not at all what one would have expected from so noble a creation as man, the creature of whom the Torah itself testified, ". . . in the image of God He created him." As we shall endeavor to illustrate, it betrays both the shame and the glory of humankind, establishing the rationale for the revelation of the Torah and the need for the formation of the chosen people of Israel.

14

Avraham was the father of that people. His life and the lives of Yizhak and Yaakov, as depicted in the Torah narrative, were glowing examples of Torah ethics and morality. And we believe that it was in order to teach mankind of the exemplary lives of our patriarchs and matriarchs that the narrative material was included in the Torah. Let us illustrate:

We will begin by posing the following question: What was it about mankind in the infancy of human history that provoked God, while our father Avraham earned only esteem and reward?

To answer this question, we must focus on three points: the creation of man, the Divine charge to him, and man's reaction to that charge. This will set the pattern for the emergence of Avraham and enable us to see his life in comparison — indeed in contrast — to those who preceded him, as well as those of his generation.

A mere perusal of the creation narrative will establish its pattern, viz., to proceed from the inanimate to the animate, the simple to the complex — from mineral to animal to man. Man, the most sophisticated of all God's creatures — indeed, the climax of creation — was made in the image of his Creator. This uncontested sophistication notwithstanding, man is recognizably animal-like in his physical properties. This is implied in the fact that he is created on the sixth day, when all the animals and beasts of the earth are also created. There is an abundance of Midrashic literature to that effect.[1] But the point is implied by the text of the Torah as well, if only by innuendo, viz., the juxtaposition of two verses: "And God said, 'Behold, I have given you all seed yielding grass upon the face of the earth and all seed yielding and fruit bearing trees for you to eat. And for all the animals of the earth

---

1. Cf. Menahem M. Kasher, "Creation and the Theory of Evolution," *Encyclopedia of Biblical Interpretation* (New York, 1953), pp. 235-241.

and all the birds of the heavens and all creeping things upon the earth that have life. All the green herbs are for all to be eaten' " (Bereshit 1:29, 30). Perhaps the juxtaposition was to humble man. Not only must he eat in order to survive, but he is so constituted that he must eat the very same food necessary to sustain the creeping things of the earth.

Yes, man is animal-like, but he is not an animal! Again, the point is not written; it is implied. After the completion of each component of creation, the Torah proclaims, "And God saw that it was good," and proceeds to the next component. On the sixth day, this statement appears after the creation of the animals, separating them categorically from man, who was created later that day. This implies the following: though physically man has many things in common with the animal kingdom, in consequence of which he was created on the sixth day, he is essentially different. Parenthetically, the proclamation does not come at all after the creation of man. We shall discuss this matter later. Finally, man alone is addressed by God; animals are not. When the Torah teaches that animals were designed to procreate, the text reads, "God blessed them, saying, 'Be fruitful and multiply, fill the waters in the seas, and let the birds increase on the earth' " (Bereshit 1:22); with regard to man, however, we read, "And God blessed them *and said to them,* 'Be fruitful and multiply, fill the earth and master it . . .' " (Bereshit 1:28).

Very much in line with what we have said are the words of Ramban:

> The correct explanation of *let us make* is as follows: It has been shown to you that God created something from nothing only on the first day, and afterwards He formed and made things from those created elements. . . . In the case of man, He said, *let us make,* i.e., I and the aforementioned earth, let us make man, the earth to bring forth the body from its elements as it did with cattle and beasts . . . and He . . . to give the spirit from His mouth. (Bereshit 1:26)

As we have said, man was created in the image of God. He was also created in the likeness of God. Although commentators differ regarding the precise meaning of these terms — to what aspect of man's uniqueness each of them refers — there is no argument against the fact that man's "spark of the Divine" is his intellect and his freedom of will — the spiritual components of his soul.

Having been completed, this unique creature called *man,* the *piece de resistance* of creation, is placed by God in the Garden of Eden and given his first test, which he fails miserably. But why? Where did he go wrong? Was it his intellect or his instincts that led him astray?

When man was created, he was a natural being, unaware of his spiritual endowment or his potential for greatness. The renowned contemporary sage and teacher par excellence Rabbi Dr. Joseph B. Soloveitchik writes:

> Natural man, unaware of the element of tension prevailing between the human being and the environment of which he is an integral part, has no need to live a normative life and to find redemption in the surrender to a higher moral will. His existence is unbounded, merging harmoniously with the general order of things and events. He is united with nature, moving straightforward with the beasts and the fowl of the field along an unbroken line of mechanical activities, never turning around . . . never glancing backwards, leading an existence which is neither fraught with contradiction, nor perplexed by paradoxes, nor marred by fright.[2]

God puts this human creature in the Garden of Eden, where he is immediately confronted with nature and the allurement of food. He sees no temptation and would surely submit to the desire to eat. But that

---

2. Joseph B. Soloveitchik, "Confrontation," *Tradition,* Vol. I No. 2, p. 6.

desire is immediately checked and set in perspective by the Divine charge not to eat from the tree of knowledge of good and evil, which stood in the middle of the garden. And thus the "ought" and "ought not" came into being. The great Spanish exegete of the 15th century Yizhak Abravanel notes that Adam did not sin out of thirst or hunger or need of any of the other necessities of life. Lust alone was his undoing.[3]

The charge to Adam not to eat from the tree of knowledge revealed to him that he had freedom of choice, that as a human being he was capable not only of *being* but of *becoming*. This is man's greatest asset. The point is made by the noted contemporary theologian Eliezer Berkovits. He writes:

> When God addressed Adam and gave him his first commandment, He called him from the innocence of complete thinghood in an eternal now into the personal reality of the not-yet, and revealed to him human freedom as the source of responsibility. Only because man is forever not-yet, because his humanity consists of self-transcendence, can he be the recipient of commandments. . . . Responsibility is the freedom of self-transcendence. Only because of that can man be entrusted with the revelation of God's word to him.[4]

By disobeying God and eating from the tree, man chose self-determination, i.e., self-determined ethics, thus setting a precedent for both himself and future generations. But it must be clearly understood that a precedent, however suggestive and foreboding, is by no means a

---

3. Cf. Yizhak Abravanel, Bereshit 2, p. 92.
4. Eliezer Berkovits, *Crisis and Faith* (New York, 1976), pp. 46-47. It is for this reason that the words "And God saw that it was good" are omitted after the creation of man. All animals actualize their potential at maturity; man is continually "becoming." Whether he is good or evil cannot be determined until his life is over.

compulsion. Besides, by limiting man's life span, God gave every generation the opportunity to start afresh. The practice of righteousness, the true knowledge of good and evil, and the obedience to God began to take root in select individuals, whose names are revealed in the Torah — Hanokh and Noah.[5] Man was not eternally damned because of the sin of Adam. In every generation, man is charged to choose "good," but the path of evil stays open to him as well, the sweet taste of forbidden fruit competing to win him over. This is the meaning of freedom.

It is important to note here that even when man chooses the path of self-determination and evil, as Adam had, he does not thereby permanently alienate his Creator. The Torah makes that point quite emphatically. After the sin and the pronouncement of punishment, we read, "And the Lord God made for man garments of skins and He dressed them" (Bereshit 3:21). Considered in its context, this is clearly an expression of love, meant to counteract any contrary, pre-conceived notions we might have about God's feelings toward Adam, his wife, and certainly subsequent generations. And should we feel that the relationship between Adam and his wife is now permanently damaged, the Torah dismisses that notion as well, by revealing to us a gracious gesture on Adam's part: "And the man called his wife Hava, for she was the mother of all living" (Bereshit 3:20). How beautiful an expression of love and understanding![6]

The path of independence and self-determination took root, developed, and spread among the early generations of man.[7] It took

---

5. Cf. David Zvi Hoffmann, Bereshit 2:9.
6. Cf. Shimshon Raphael Hirsch, *Commentary on the Torah*, trans. Isaac Levy (London, 1959), Bereshit 3:20.
7. Cf. *Bereshit Rabbah* 38. In the generation of Enosh, God destroyed a third of the world, but the people did not learn their lesson.

root in Cain who, in a fit of anger, killed his brother Abel. To show his defiance of God and his lack of responsibility toward anyone but himself, he exclaimed, "Am I my brother's keeper?" Ten generations later, in the time of Noah, the world had so corrupted itself that God decreed its destruction. And if we were to ask, "Why destroy this world only to create another?" the answer would be, "because of Noah." Were it not for the life that he lived, there would have been no purpose in destroying mankind. For if all men had freely chosen to be evil, it would have established beyond question that there was something basically wrong with either the design of man or the environment in which he lived. To recreate man in the same pattern would have eventually resulted in the same problem, and thus have been purposeless. Because Noah found favor in God's eyes, the world was destroyed, for it proved that man was capable of redemption — that he was *not* so constituted that he would consistently choose evil. As such, there was hope for mankind.

One would certainly have expected that the new world — i.e., the civilization that developed after the Flood — would be a changed world. Regrettably, it was not. The Midrash teaches that Shem, the son of Noah, had set up a school to teach righteousness, but no others are thus singled out. It would seem that self-determined ethics began to triumph once more. This is graphically depicted in the story of the Tower of Babel.

The goal of the tower builders was to make for themselves a name. They would build a great city, and in its center they would erect a tower that would reach to heaven.[8] Why to heaven? Rashi explains: "They came with one plan, saying, 'He has no right to select the heavenly

---

8. Cf. Bereshit 11:1-8.

regions exclusively for Himself; let us ascend to the sky and make war upon Him!' "[9] It seems that there is no limit to the self-deception and sheer audacity to which the godless stoop. Truly, they had even another motive in building the city. The Almighty had commanded them to be fruitful and multiply so that they would fill the earth. They showed their defiance of God's command. They would gather together in a city which would unite them, rather than spread across the land. The city would also protect them from another cataclysmic event such as the Flood . . . a grim prospect that must surely have entered their minds. But how? An excellent point is made by Joseph B. Soloveitchik on this matter:

> The root of the instinct of gregariousness which is the very foundation of the natural community is to be found already in the animal kingdom. Let cattle grazing quietly along a wide area of green pastures sense suddenly that danger is lurking somewhere, they — overcome by instinctive panic — will begin to herd together and cling to each other as if mere physical contiguity could avert the impending catastrophe. The difference between man associating with others and animals flocking together consists, of course, in the fact that while the mute creatures react in a mechanical, spurious, and purposeless way, eloquent and wise man acts intelligently.[10]

As with the generation of the Flood, self-determined subjective ethics, rather than binding the people to each other, serve to alienate them — indeed, pit them against one another — and human life becomes dispensable. It is the classic example of egocentricity taken to its ultimate conclusion.

---

9. *Ibid.,* 11:1
10. J.B. Soloveitchik, "The Lonely Man of Faith," *Tradition,* Vol. 7 No. 2, p. 20.

True, by confusing their language God didn't uproot their philosophy, but He did thwart their efforts, and so they abandoned the perverse project.

This is the milieu into which Avraham was born.

Chapter 1

Avraham and Sarah

It has been a common practice among Torah commentators to compare and contrast Noah with Avraham. Perhaps the most famous of such commentators is Rashi. On the verse "These are the generations of Noah; Noah was a righteous man; he was blameless in his age; Noah walked with God" (Bereshit 6:9), Rashi comments:

> Some of our Rabbis explain it to his credit: he was righteous even in his generation; it follows that, had he lived in a generation of righteous people, he would have been even more righteous. Others, however, explain it to his discredit: in comparison with his own generation, he was accounted righteous, but had he lived in the generation of Avraham, he would have been accounted as of no importance.

Noah was primarily concerned with himself; Avraham was interested in all of mankind. Perhaps this is why God selected Avraham to be the father of a nation whose mission was to bring mankind back to God. The point of eliteness is made by the brilliant Talmudic scholar and Torah commentator of 19th century Germany David Zvi Hoffmann, who writes:

> After most of society turned away from God, the Divine will at first saw fit to quell the spreading of this evil throughout society by

23

confusing the language of the people. Then the Divine will appointed Avraham to be the founder of a nation that would actualize His plan to bring mankind back to Him.

(Bereshit 12:1)

How did Avraham come to monotheism?

From the Midrash it is clear that Avraham's concern with God did not begin with *revelation,* but rather with *speculation* — an intellectual gesture, a process of discovery that unfolds and builds gradually. Perhaps his predisposition to speculation was due to the intellectual climate of the city of his birth, Ur of the Chaldeans. Archeology gives us a picture of this city in the time of Avraham. Although there was widespread polytheism, we have evidence that general elementary education was widespread there as well. Many were able to read and write and do simple arithmetic. The more advanced studied practical geometry.[11]

The postdiluvian patriarchs, i.e., Noah, Shem, and Ever, became links between the early generations and Avraham, for the traditions about God and the history of early times were handed down by them. Avraham knew the stories of creation, the Garden of Eden, the Flood, and the Tower of Babel. He knew the seven Noahide commandments and the genealogical tables of descent from Adam. The noted contemporary scholar Philip Biberfeld writes:

> All these traditions were the common inheritance of all the descendants of Noah. But . . . they had become corrupted and mixed with mythical and polytheistic elements. The Hebrew traditions retained the simple, original purity, which fixes them as

---

11. Cf. Philip Biberfeld, *Universal Jewish History* (New York, 1948), Vol. I, p. 119.

closer to the source than the versions of the other peoples.[12]

The Midrash is most enlightening with regard to Avraham's speculation. We read:

> It may be likened to a person who went from place to place and once came upon a lighted palace. He said to the one who had accompanied him, "Would you say that the palace has no master?" The master immediately came forth and said, "I am the master of this palace." So did Avraham say, "Do you think there is no Master of the world?" The Master immediately came forth and said, "I am the Master of the world."
>
> (Bereshit Rabbah 39)

This is the familiar teleological proof for the existence of God: the argument from design. According to the Midrash, it was the vehicle through which Avraham came to an understanding of God and the argument he presented to others. A somewhat different approach to this Midrash is taken by Yizhak Arama, the 15th century Spanish sage and exegete:

Avraham went from place to place, i.e., from the primitive to the sophisticated levels of understanding. His speculation led him to astrology, the movement and positions of the stars — depicted in the Midrash as the "lighted palace." Avraham knew that the stars moved, and he proposed that an object that is itself moved cannot be the original mover. A Prime Mover must exist that has set all things into motion, one which is itself unmoved. This Prime Mover is God. No sooner did Avraham reach this level of understanding than the spirit of God came upon him, saying, "Go forth from your native land . . ."

---

12. *Ibid.*, pp. 121-122.

This is implied in the words of the Midrash, "The Master immediately came forth and said, 'I am the Master of the world.' "[13]

To test his faith and prime him for the fatherhood of the nation of Israel, Avraham was put through ten trials. Had he failed in any of these trials, God might have selected another to take his place. But Avraham did not falter; he remained steadfast in his faith and commitment.

The first trial was the command that he leave his home and set forth for a new land, a place that was not familiar to him: the land of Canaan. Aside from the journey — in itself fraught with danger — he knew nothing of what might happen there. But he obeyed. The second trial was the famine forcing him to journey to Egypt for food. The third trial was his experience in Egypt; his life was threatened and his wife was taken captive by Pharaoh. The fourth trial was the war of four kings against five, a battle which he was forced to enter in order to save his nephew Lot. The fifth trial was taking Hagar as a concubine to give him the child his wife Sarah was unable to bear. The sixth trial was circumcision. The seventh trial was the taking of Sarah by Avimelekh, king of Gerar. The eighth trial was the dismissal of Hagar. The ninth trial was the dismissal of Yishmael. The tenth trial was the binding of Yizhak.

Each of these experiences in its own right would have been enough to discourage and dissuade a person of lesser character from his faith and trust in God. Such a person would undoubtedly have reasoned: "I am obviously in error in my thinking. An ethical God would not have allowed me to suffer so much in fulfilling His commands." But Avraham did not veer one degree from the course God had charted for him. His experiences actualized his potential as "God's faithful

---

13. Cf. Yizhak Arama, *Akedat Yizhak,* Bereshit, *Sha'ar* 16, p. 117.

servant," a phrase used many years later by the Prophet Yeshayahu to depict the nation of Israel.

Let us backtrack and examine some of these experiences more carefully. Avraham went from one level to the next, not only in his discovery of God but in his faith as well — from a life of searching to a life of supreme trust and unqualified commitment. God had promised Avraham that he would have a son, an heir to continue his spiritual work. But Avraham and Sarah were barren for many years. When God reiterated the promise to Avraham, Sarah was somewhat skeptical — due to their age — but Avraham was confident. He trusted in God and knew that the promise would eventually be fulfilled despite their advanced years. As the Torah clearly records, "And he (Avraham) had faith in the Lord, and He (God) counted it to him as righteousness" (Bereshit 15:6).

When well along in years, Avraham was charged with a commandment that was to become the medal of honor of the nation of Israel and the medium through which they would enter into a covenant with God — the mitzvah of circumcision. Avraham was most apprehensive regarding this commandment, because he felt that it would become a wall of separation between himself and the nations. His noble mission to perfect the world by bringing mankind to ethical monotheism would be thwarted. Indeed, before he was circumcised, all passers-by would stop at his tent, where he would offer them food and teach them about God; afterwards, they seldom came by. What he had not realized, however, was that this was exactly what God wanted — not that they should withdraw from him, but that he should withdraw from them. For God had initiated a profound change in Avraham with the mitzvah of circumcision — both a physical and a spiritual change. God now directed him to his most essential task in life. From this point on, Avraham would no longer be involved in the perfection of humanity at large; he would concentrate his efforts on self-perfection and the perfection of his family, the future patriarchs and matriarchs of Israel.[14]

To what extent had Avraham been involved with humanity, and how did this role now change?

When Avraham's beliefs and commitment had been firmly established in his mind, he began to preach to the people of Ur, his birthplace. In view of the fact that Ur of the Chaldeans was a city notoriously polytheistic, it is not surprising that his ideas were not well received.[15] The Midrash records that it led to his imprisonment by King Nimrod.[16] What occurred afterwards is subject to controversy, however. According to Rashi, Nimrod had Avraham thrown into a fiery furnace. A miracle saved his life.[17] Rabbi Moshe, son of Maimon (Maimonides), and others hold that Nimrod banished Avraham from Ur as a punishment for his preaching.[18]

It was the Divine plan that brought Avraham to Canaan. There he could continue to develop spiritually, devoting himself to his noble mission. As the Midrash explains, "The Holy One Blessed Be He said to Avraham, 'Rather than enlightening Mesopotamia and its environs, come and enlighten the people in the land of Israel.' "[19]

It is interesting to note that the sacred work in which Avraham was engaged is merely alluded to in the text. The Torah refers to the

---

14. Meir M'eeri, *Torah Me'irah* (London, 1960), Bereshit 12:1, p. 3.
15. Moshe Maimonides, *Mishneh Torah:* Laws Concerning Idolatry 1:3.
16. Cf. *Bereshit Rabbah* 38:19.
17. Bereshit 11:28.
18. M. Maimonides, *Guide of the Perplexed,* trans. M. Friedlander (New York, Hebrew Publishing Co.), Part III, Chapter 29.
19. *Bereshit Rabbah* 30:11.

construction of altars where Avraham called upon the name of God.[20] Avraham would enter a town, and with the permission of the townspeople build an altar and preach to them. When he was reasonably assured that his teachings were accepted — i.e., that the people had relinquished their idolatrous beliefs — he would leave the town, and the altar would remain as a testimony to his work.[21]

Avraham's concern and involvement with humanity was not limited to his preaching. He felt a strong responsibility to save them from the wrath and punishment of God. After all, God had Himself said of him, "All the families of the earth shall bless themselves by you." An excellent example of such involvement is the story of the destruction of Sodom.[22]

What was the sin of Sodom, and why did Avraham feel compelled to get involved?

The people of Sodom sinned not only against God, but against their fellow man. What was worse, they built their wickedness into the law of the land. According to the Midrash, it had been decreed in Sodom that whoever supports the poor would be sentenced to death. Plotit, the daughter of Lot, had been so accused, and she was taken to be burned at the stake. In despair, she raised her voice to God, crying, "Master of the world, avenge me." Her cry rose before the Throne of Glory. Said the Holy One Blessed Be He: "I will go down and see whether the people of Sodom are guilty, as the outcry that has come before Me indicates. If they are, I will overturn the city."[23]

---

20. Cf. Bereshit 12:8, 13:4, 8.
21. Cf. Yaakov Zvi Mecklenberg, *Ha-Ketav V'ha-Kabbalah* (New York, 1946), Bereshit 12:7.
22. Cf. Bereshit 18 and 19.
23. Pirke D'Rabbi Eliezer 25. Cf. also Bereshit 18:21.

When a society has so degenerated that immorality is incorporated into the constitution and the citizens fail to protest, there is no hope for its survival. It will either be destroyed by God or it will destroy itself. As we know, the former option was its destiny. But why? Perhaps the words of Maimonides will serve to enlighten us somewhat on this matter:

> Every man must see himself throughout the year as evenly balanced between innocence and guilt, and look upon the entire world as if it is evenly balanced between innocence and guilt; thus, if he commits one sin, he will overbalance himself and the whole world to the side of guilt, and be a cause of its destruction. But if he performs one duty, he will overbalance himself and the whole world to the side of virtue, and bring about his own and its salvation and escape.[24]

Though Maimonides is speaking generally and hypothetically, it is quite possible that such has been the case many times in history. And although Maimonides does not mean to imply that God operates by strict mathematics, there may very well be situations where it boils down to just that. Perhaps Sodom was such a situation. The single act of wickedness perpetrated against Plotit may have tipped the scales, spelling out doom for the city.

Sodom was about to be destroyed. Yet, before God did so, He revealed His plan to Avraham. Why? The Torah explains: "And the Lord said: 'Shall I hide from Avraham what I am about to do, since Avraham is to become a great and populous nation and all the nations of the earth are to bless themselves by him?' " (Bereshit 18:18). The world would be blessed by Avraham's presence, for he was concerned

---

24. M. Maimonides, *Mishneh Torah,* Laws Concerning Repentance 3:4.

with all of mankind. Every human being was precious to him. It was as though God felt a responsibility, so to speak, to inform Avraham so that he would plead in their behalf.

Avraham prepared for the task. He undoubtedly thought the matter through very carefully. He was well aware of the shortcomings of his forefather Noah, who had not taken sufficient interest in his fellow man. Indeed, had the latter done so, he might have saved the world from the Flood.

"Avraham drew near . . ." the Torah tells us. Rashi comments: "The phrase *to draw near* is used in the Torah to indicate drawing near to make battle, to appease, and to pray. With regard to Avraham, it implies all three" (Bereshit 18:23).

Let us examine the text of Avraham's conversation with the Almighty with regard to the city of Sodom.

And Avraham drew near and said, "Will You sweep away the innocent along with the guilty? What if there should be fifty innocent within the city? Will You then wipe out the place and not forgive it for the sake of the innocent fifty who are in it? Far be it for You to do such a thing, to bring death upon the innocent as well as the guilty, so that the innocent and the guilty fare alike. Far be it from You! Shall not the Judge of all the earth deal justly?" And the Lord answered, "If I find within the city of Sodom fifty innocent ones, I will forgive the whole place for their sake." Avraham spoke up, saying, "Here I venture to speak to the Lord — I, who am but dust and ashes: What if the fifty innocent shall lack five? Will You destroy the whole city for want of five?" And He answered, "I will not destroy if I find forty-five there." But he spoke to Him again and said, "What if forty should be found there?" And He answered, "I will not do it for the sake of the forty." And he said, "Let not the Lord be angry if I go on: What if thirty should be found there?" And He answered, "I will not do it if I find thirty there." And he said, "I venture again to speak to the Lord: What if twenty should be found there?" And He answered, "I will not destroy for the sake of the

31

twenty." And he said, "Let not the Lord be angry if I speak but this last time: What if ten should be found there?" And He answered, "I will not destroy for the sake of the ten."

(Bereshit 18:23-32)

Avraham offered two arguments: justice and mercy. First, would it be an act of justice for God to execute the wicked together with the righteous? Would this not imply that there is no morality in the Heavenly Court? If there were only ten righteous men in the city, a minimum number to be sure, should they be killed with the wicked? Is that justice? Second, couldn't the wicked be spared in merit of the righteous? As such, the righteous would also benefit, for they would have that much more time to reach out to the wicked and win them over.[25]

Much to Avraham's dismay, there were not even ten righteous men in the city. He had succeeded in his plea, but the city of Sodom could not meet even the minimal requirements, and so it was destroyed.

Avraham and Lot

The Torah's record of Avraham's life is certainly not limited to examples of his concern for mankind alone; it reveals his devotion to family as well. Of particular interest is his relationship with Lot, his nephew, for when he left for the land of Canaan he took Lot with him. Two verses allude to the fact that what began as a gesture of good will and familial responsibility on Avraham's part degenerated into estrangement and friction between the two men, and ultimately resulted in their separation.

When he left Haran, the Torah records: "Avram went forth as the Lord had spoken with him . . . Avram took his wife Sarai *and his*

---

25. Eliezer Ashkenazi, *Ma'ase Hashem* (Jerusalem, 1972), Bereshit, VaYera 17.

nephew Lot and all the wealth that they had gathered, and the persons that they had acquired in Haran, and they set out for the land of Canaan" (Bereshit 12:4, 5). A famine in Canaan forced Avraham to leave the land and sojourn in Egypt. When he left, the Torah records: "From Egypt, Avram went up into the Negev, with his wife and all that he possessed, *together with Lot*" (Bereshit 13:1).

If we compare the order in which Lot appears in the verses above, we will note that when they started out the two men were one family; when they left Egypt, however, they were two somewhat estranged relatives. There can be no other explanation for the change in the verses. But we must ask: What was responsible for this estrangement? Could it have been the fact that when they left Egypt Lot had already acquired his own wealth and, with it, a sense of independence? Note the verse: "And Lot, who went with Avram, also had flocks and herds and tents" (Bereshit 13:5), and Rashi's comment: "Who brought it about that he possessed all this? It was the fact that he accompanied Avraham."

The estrangement of the two men finally led to their separation. And though it was Avraham who initiated the action, it was predicated on Lot's unethical behavior. Avraham had good intentions when he took Lot with him to Canaan. He had hoped to influence Lot to accept monotheism and live the ethical and moral life. When Avraham left Egypt there was still some hope that they could live together as a family, but that soon changed.

There is no better example of Lot's perverse thinking than the incident of the shepherds' quarreling.[26] Here it is important to recognize that it was not the shepherds' arguments that were being put forth —

---

26. Bereshit 13:5-7.

for what difference would it make to them? — but rather the opinions of Avraham and Lot, their masters. Rashi explains that Lot's shepherds were grazing their animals in fields that belonged to others. When rebuked by the shepherds of Avraham, they argued that the land had been promised to Avraham. Since he had no son, Lot would be his heir. As such, the land was technically theirs, so there was nothing wrong with taking it now.[27]

The land issue was the immediate cause of the separation — the last straw. But there were ideological differences as well between the two men.[28] And so, Avraham turns to Lot with the words: "Let there be no strife between you and me, between my shepherds and yours, for we are kinsmen. Is not the whole land before you? Let us separate. If you go north, I will go south; if you go south, I will go north" (Bereshit 13:8, 9).

Though Avraham is the greater and the more accomplished of the two men, he gives Lot the choice of land, as a gesture of kindness. One might have expected Lot to insist that Avraham make the first choice. After all, Lot owed all his material possessions to Avraham. But Lot was a self-determined man whose decisions were based first and foremost on self-interest. He was a "taker," not a "giver." How artfully the Torah portrays Lot's thinking as he makes the choice: "And Lot lifted his eyes and saw how well watered was the whole plain of the Jordan, all of it — this was before the Lord had destroyed Sodom and Amorrah — all the way to Zoar, like the garden of the Lord, like the land of Egypt. So Lot chose for himself the whole plain of the Jordan, and Lot journeyed eastward. Thus they parted from each other" (Bereshit 13:10-12).

---

27. *Ibid.,* Rashi commentary.
28. Cf. *Bereshit Rabbah* 38.7.

How reminiscent are these words of another important choice portrayed in the Torah, the one made by Adam and Hava. "And the woman saw that the tree was good for eating, a delight to the eyes, and that the tree was desirable as a source of wisdom, and she took of its fruit and did eat . . ." (Bereshit 3:6). How similar are the language and considerations. Indeed, in both cases, the eye sees and the heart lusts!

But Avraham was not Lot. Although the two had separated, Avraham would not relinquish his responsibilities to his nephew. Lot was still family. Besides, Avraham had promised Lot that he would be at his side if Lot needed him.[29] Avraham had only to hear that Lot was in danger, and he responded.

Avraham and Sarah

There is no doubt that the relationship between Avraham and Sarah was unique. Here again Avraham departed from the thinking and culture of his time. Sarah was not only his wife; she was his partner, his equal, and, at times, his superior. It must have been a marriage that was rooted in great intellectual and spiritual compatibility.

This compatibility is first alluded to in a textual redundancy. The Torah records: "And Avram and Nahor took for themselves wives. The name of Avram's wife was Sarai and the name of the wife of Nahor was Milcah, daughter of Haran — *who was the father of Milcah and the father of Yiscah*" (Bereshit 11:29). This is followed by the statement: "And Sarai was barren, childless." Now, if Milcah was the daughter of Haran, Haran was obviously her father. Why the redundancy? Secondly, who was Yiscah? She is never mentioned in the text again. Here Rashi enlightens us: "Yiscah, this was Sarai; she was named

---

29. Cf. Rashi, Bereshit 13:9.

Yiscah (from a root meaning 'to see') because she could see the future by Divine inspiration . . ." The seemingly redundant phrase is actually there to teach us that Milcah and Yiscah were sisters. But it is also to teach us that Sarah was a woman endowed with exceptional intellectual and spiritual qualities.

What is interesting is that immediately following the Torah's allusion to Sarah's spiritual excellence we are told that she was barren. What does this connote if not that the marriage of Avraham and Sarah drew much of its strength from their spiritual compatibility and the calling they shared — a calling which, by Divine plan and design, would substitute for the joy and responsibility they could have shared had they been blessed with a large family? This relationship and joint calling is alluded to in the Torah and spelled out by Rashi. We thus read:

> And Avram took Sarai his wife, and Lot his nephew, and all their substance that they had gathered, and the *souls that they had made* in Haran, and they went forth to go into the land of Canaan.
> (Bereshit 12:5)
>
> Rashi: The souls which he had brought under the wings of the Divine Presence. Avraham converted the men and Sarah converted the women, and Scripture accounts it to them as if they had made them.

Avraham regarded Sarah as an equal. When she showed superior judgment, emotional detachment, and objectivity in times of crisis, he accepted her opinion and followed her advice. There are two such examples recorded in the Torah:

Sarah had not given Avraham the son God had promised would be his heir. Many years had passed, and Sarah began to feel that it was not her destiny to bear that child. Knowing full well, however, that God's promise had to be fulfilled, she advised Avraham to take Hagar, her handmaid, as a concubine. Reluctantly Avraham heeded her advice.[30] She gave the instructions and he obeyed. Interestingly, the Midrash alludes to the fact that God Himself approved of Sarah's words.[31]

Hagar then bore Avraham a son, who was named Yishmael. Much to Avraham's dismay, however, Yishmael did not seem to be his spiritual heir. Eventually, Sarah, too, was blessed with a son, Yizhak. Both Hagar and Yishmael taunted Yizhak. Sarah saw this, and it distressed her. She advised Avraham to send Hagar and Yishmael away, for she felt that Yishmael had no moral right to inherit the spiritual and material blessings alongside Yizhak. Once again Sarah exercised sound, practical judgment. Once again Avraham obeyed, despite his hesitation at first, for once again God had given His approval. As the Torah records: "But God said to Avraham, 'Do not be distressed over the boy or your slave; whatever Sarah tells you, do as she says, for it is through Yizhak that your offspring shall be continued' " (Bereshit 21:12).

Avraham's high regard for Sarah, viz., her welfare and her honor, motivated him to devise a plan for their travels which would afford her ample protection. Wherever they went, he told her to identify herself as his sister. Whether this is to be understood as the wife-sister status known in the Hurrian society of that time, endowing a wife with special privileges not enjoyed by most women in that culture, or simply as a ploy to avoid trouble, it was done as a precautionary measure. Avraham was greatly concerned with what might happen to them as strangers in an unknown country.[32] Considering that Sarah was a

---

30. Cf. Ramban, Bereshit 16:2.
31. *Bereshit Rabbah* 45:3. The Midrash reads: "And Avram hearkened unto Sarai's voice" (Bereshit 16:2). Said R. Yose: The voice of Divine Inspiration."
32. Cf. Nahum Sarna, *Understanding Genesis* (New York, 1972), pp. 102-103.

beautiful woman, the possibility that they would be apprehended — he killed and she taken captive — was not at all remote. Indeed, in those societies, it may very well have been the rule rather than the exception. If, on the other hand, they were brother and sister traveling together, their parents would have given him the responsibility for her welfare. If someone would be interested in Sarah, he would be required to negotiate with Avraham for her, an alternative Avraham would certainly have preferred to unnecessary bloodshed. Now, a woman of Sarah's endowments could command a high price — much too high for most people to even consider. As such, they could both be spared; he from harm, she from dishonor.

When a famine struck the land of Canaan, forcing Avraham and Sarah to sojourn to Egypt, they invoked this plan. Although it may very well have worked at other times, it did not succeed in Egypt. Avraham had not anticipated that Pharaoh himself would seek to purchase Sarah, and could do so for whatever price Avraham demanded.[33]

Despite its logic, the plan was problematic. No matter how she identified herself, wasn't Sarah still married to Avraham? If she was taken and violated, she would experience the guilt of having committed an extramarital act. What, then, did Avraham expect to accomplish with the plan "Say you are my sister"?

Maimonides teaches that before the giving of the Torah there was no marriage ceremony. When a couple wished to marry, they would live together, thus consummating the marriage. If they wished to end the relationship, they would simply separate; there were no legal documents of divorce.[34] Although Avraham fulfilled the entire Torah, in extenuating circumstances he would abide by the Noahide laws. If

---

33. Cf. E. Ashkenazi, *Ma'ase Hashem, op. cit.,* Ma'ase Avot Chapter 4.
34. Cf. M. Maimonides, *Mishneh Torah:* Laws Concerning Marriage 1:1.

they came to a place where Sarah was in danger of being violated, they would consider themselves to have separated. As a single woman, there would be no problem of extramarital relations. Understandably, when they left the town he would remarry her.[35]

Sarah, the First Matriarch

What was it about the personality of Sarah that made her so compatible with Avraham?

When Sarah died, the Torah records: "And the life of Sarah was a hundred years and twenty years and seven years; these were the years of the life of Sarah" (Bereshit 23:1). Although the accepted translation of the last phrase is "the years of the life of Sarah," as we have written, the Hebrew could be translated: "the two lives of Sarah," and some have indeed rendered it so. As such, the words would be particularly relevant to the life she led and most complimentary to her.

This point is made by the 19th century renowned German sage and exegete par excellence Yaakov Zvi Mecklenberg. Man is a most unique creature. He is the only creation who has been endowed by the Almighty with spiritual as well as physical properties. By virtue of this blend, Man has been charged to live two lives: a physical life and a spiritual life. Both are to be lived in accordance with Divine law, harmoniously blended together as one — unified and inseparable. Few and far between are those who are known to have actualized this goal in their lives. Sarah is one of them.[36]

Our Sages have testified that both the physical and the spiritual facets of her life were lived according to the highest and noblest ideals

---

35. Cf. Y.Z. Mecklenberg, *op. cit.,* Bereshit 12:13.
36. *Ibid.,* 23:1.

of Torah. Sarah lived two lives; she was a mother and a matriarch. She was Avraham's wife and the mother of his son Yizhak. She fulfilled all the necessary duties incumbent upon a wife and mother. But she was also a woman with a spiritual calling. Her spiritual role began as soon as she married Avraham, but her motherly role began much later. As a woman, she was deeply distressed and impatient regarding this misfortune. When she bade Avraham to take Hagar, she had a twofold purpose in mind. First and foremost, she wanted to facilitate God's promise to Avraham that he would have a son. Second, she wanted to taste the joys of motherhood, for she was convinced that Hagar would be honored to allow her to raise the child in accordance with the Avrahamite tradition.[37]

A son was born to Avraham and Hagar. However, just as it was not Yishmael's destiny to be Avraham's heir, so was he not destined to be raised by Sarah. Sarah had erred in her thinking. Despite the apparent closeness of the two women when they left Egypt, the birth of Yishmael initiated a profound change in their relationship.[38] Perhaps the very idea that Hagar would allow Sarah to raise the child was mere wishful thinking on Sarah's part. It would seem that despite the years Hagar had spent with Avraham and Sarah, and her long exposure to their way of life and religious beliefs, she lacked their dedication and was not at all sensitive to their mission.

There is one other facet of the situation to be considered here. Hagar was the daughter of Pharaoh. True, when she left Egypt to become a member of Avraham's household, she was prepared to be a servant — even a slave — but the situation had changed. As the mother of Avraham's only heir, she may now have envisioned herself once more a

---

37. Cf. Y. Abravanel, Bereshit 16:1.
38. Cf. M. M'eeri, *op. cit.,* Bereshit 16:1.

royal princess — indeed, the first matriarch of the Jewish people, deserving of the right to stand highest in rank at Avraham's side. Hence, Sarah's thinking was utterly repugnant to her. The point is not at all remote. On the contrary, it is alluded to in the Torah and confirmed by the words of Rashi. We read:

> And he cohabited with Hagar and she conceived; and when she saw that she had conceived, her mistress was lowered in her esteem.
> (Bereshit 16:4)
>
> Rashi: She said, "As regards this woman, Sarah, her conduct in private can certainly not be like that in public. She pretends to be a righteous woman, but she cannot really be righteous, since all these years she has not been privileged to have children, while I have had that blessing from the first union."

How quickly success changes friend to foe! We must take note, however, that Nahmanides takes a very strong stand against Sarah. Opening his remarks with the words "Sarah our mother sinned," Nahmanides argues that if Sarah was unable to anticipate the consequences and learn to live with them she should never have given Hagar to Avraham. Thus, her suggestion that Hagar be sent away was not only harsh; it was improper. Despite Nahmanides, however, one might argue that Sarah's error in judgment was due to her belief in Hagar's altruism, a common foible of the righteous.

Notwithstanding all we have said, Sarah still longed for a son of her own. Perhaps if Yishmael had been a true son to Avraham, a worthy heir to his spiritual mission, she would have accepted her lot in life. But this was simply not the case. When her son was born, therefore, she was ecstatic. Indeed, the world would share her happiness. And she exclaimed: "God has brought me laughter; everyone who hears will laugh with me" (Bereshit 21:6).

A rather interesting approach to the name Yizhak is taken by Joseph B. Soloveitchik. The very idea that a son would walk in his father's footsteps was laughable to the people of that era — particularly when to do so would be to promote so strange an ideal as ethical monotheism. But Yizhak would mock them as a living testimony to the ideal relationship between father and son. He would prove that what was considered laughable and indeed impossible had in fact been successfully accomplished by Avraham and Yizhak, despite the generation gap between them. What once engendered laughter in the eyes of the masses would henceforth engender awe and admiration.[39]

The Binding of Yizhak

We now move to an event which was undoubtedly the most difficult and traumatic experience in the lives of Avraham and Yizhak, and perhaps the most enigmatic event in Biblical history: the binding of Yizhak.

What were some of the complexities that marked this event?

Avraham related to Yizhak on two levels: as a father and as a mentor. Both were of crucial significance here. True, without a son, none of the promises God had made to Avraham could have been fulfilled. But it was not merely the fulfillment of promises that Avraham sought; it was also the joy and pride in being a father. In this regard, he was no different than Sarah. This point is alluded to in the Torah. When God reassures him that his reward will be great, Avraham responds: "O Lord God, what can You give me, since I go childless . . ." (Bereshit 15:2). His feelings are reaffirmed when Yizhak is born and the Torah records: "The child grew up and was weaned and Avraham held a great feast on the day that Yizhak was

---

39. Cf. J.B. Soloveitchik, *Hamesh Drashot* (Jerusalem, 1974), pp. 70-71.

weaned" (Bereshit 21:8). With Yizhak, Avraham was fulfilled. Then came the perplexing command and the equally perplexing response:

> And it came to pass after these things that God tested Avraham and said to him, "Avraham." And he said, "Behold, here I am." And He said, "Take now your son, your only one, whom you love, Yizhak, and go into the land of Moriah, and bring him up there for a burnt offering upon one of the mountains, which I will identify to you."
>
> (Bereshit 22:2)

Avraham was a man of unqualified and uncompromising faith in God. Until this point in his life, there was never any conflict between what he understood as ethical and moral and what was revealed to him to be God's will. He preached ethical monotheism: God is One; God is Good; the only sacrifice God wants of man is that he commit himself to worship and to ethical behavior toward his fellow man. For the non-Jew, this meant and still means commitment to the seven Noahide laws. For Avraham and his family at that time, and for the Jews once the Torah was revealed, this meant commitment to the 613 commandments.

Avraham preached that God detests human sacrifice, that there is nothing more sacred and of greater value than a human life. Then came the revelation that he was to bring his son Yizhak as a sacrifice to this God. How incongruous! And there was yet another dilemma with which Avraham wrestled: the revealed word of God contradicted reason. On the one hand it was revealed to Avraham that Yizhak was to be his heir, and on the other that he was to be brought as a sacrifice.

What were Avraham's alternatives and their implications?

To heed God's command meant to disregard reason in an act of unqualified submission to God's will. It was to accept God's law as a *hok,* an incomprehensible statute. But even more was implied. To submit meant not only to accept and follow the incomprehensible; it meant to act contrary to a cardinal principle of his life's teaching: the sacredness of human life and its supremacy over all other considerations.

The alternative position was to refuse to obey God's command. It could be rationalized on two counts. First, to Avraham's way of thinking, the act was immoral. Second, it contradicted God's promise that Yizhak would be Avraham's heir.

What the matter boiled down to was man's apparently eternal dilemma: revelation versus reason.

Avraham's immediate response to God's call was *hineni,* i.e., I am here and ready to obey. In light of the fact that he had not yet heard the command, his statement reflects an attitude of unqualified commitment — much like that of the nation of Israel who, close to 400 years later, committed themselves to the Torah with the words: "All that the Lord has spoken we will do" (Shemot 19:8).

But what was Avraham's reaction the following morning, after he had time to consider the matter? "And Avraham arose in the morning, saddled his ass, and took with him two of his servants and his son Yizhak. He split the wood for the burnt offering, and he set out for the place of which God had told him" (Bereshit 22:3).

What a night that must have been. How Avraham must have struggled with his conscience! But by morning all was resolved, for the language of the Torah reflects a manner that was forthright, resolute, and unhesitant. Avraham proceeded from one move to the next, methodically and apparently uninhibitedly.

What of Yizhak? We must keep in mind that he was no child; he was a mature thirty-seven-year-old. In truth, it was his trial as well. At the outset of the journey to Moriah, Avraham knew what had to be done, but Yizhak did not. At that point the text reads: "And they went both of them together." Father and son were one in their conformity with God's word. But even after Yizhak's probing, when he realized that *he* was to be the sacrifice to the Lord, the Torah repeats, "And they went both of them together." Clearly, the devastating truth did not in any way affect his trust in his father Avraham or his love of, and devotion to, God. What was to be done had to be done. It was God's will.

What did the trial of Avraham prove, and for whom?

Nothing needs to be proved to God the Omniscient One. The trial was to enrich Avraham and, through him, all those who would learn of his deed. Avraham was a self-made man; a probing thinker and philosopher, he had the courage to swim against the tide and make substantial strides in the discovery of truth. Avraham was unique; he stood alone. The only prophet in Israel who exceeded his stature was Moses. Nevertheless, he was a human being — mortal and finite, and thus imperfect. For his own well being, he had to be shown that there are some things beyond even his comprehension. Even more importantly, Avraham had to actualize his faith potential by demonstrating that his ultimate commitment was to God. Although the other nine trials had established this to some extent, they were logical and reasonable, and that made a profound difference. The binding of Yizhak was irrational, or perhaps suprarational — certainly beyond his understanding. Conformity with the Divine charge was a definitive statement. It postulated that for the man of faith revelation supersedes reason — that obedience is predicated solely on the fact that it is the Divine will. As such, Avraham's obedience to the charge that he bring Yizhak as an offering was the ultimate sanctification of God's name, for his own generation and for posterity as well.[40]

---

40. Cf. Joseph Albo, *Sefer ha-Ikkarim,* Ma'amar V, Chapter 23; also Y.Z. Mecklenberg, *op. cit.,* Bereshit 22:1.

A most interesting approach to this question is taken by Joseph B. Soloveitchik. The religious act is primarily an experience of suffering. God demands self-sacrifice in the realm of man's most basic physical drives. He imposes upon man's freedom, charging him with a transcendental norm that renounces excessive preoccupation with the flesh and at times even the pursuit of pleasure. Man must bring sacrifices. This is a fundamental charge to the religionist. God demands of Avraham the ultimate sacrifice — a gesture that would render Avraham alone and barren, indeed, forever plagued by incomparable loneliness. Understandably, the culmination of man's self-sacrifice, which begins with suffering and trembling, is eternal joy. When Avraham removed his son from the altar by decree of the angel, his suffering turned to eternal joy and his trembling to eternal tranquility. The religious act always begins with self-sacrifice, but ends with self-discovery. There is no self-discovery without self-sacrifice, for man can only find that which he had once lost.[41]

---

41. Cf. J.B. Soloveitchik, *B'sod ha-Yahid V'ha-Yahad,* ed. Pinhas Peli (Jerusalem, 1975), pp. 427-428.

Chapter 2

Yizhak and Rivkah

At the very moment he was conceived, Yizhak, the second of the patriarchs, testified to the omnipotence, faithfulness, and ultimate concern of the Almighty for those who trust in Him. Yizhak, literally, "laughter," symbolized God's laughter at those who deny His existence, His power, and His concern for man. Having been conceived by Avraham and Sarah in their old age, Yizhak testified to the fact that at times God contravenes the laws of nature and performs miracles. Indeed, this initial Divine act on behalf of Avraham set a precedent that would apply to the relationship of God with the Jewish people for all time.[42]

In a sense, the name bespoke the man. Yizhak became interested in nature and involved with its metaphysical implications. Quite possibly, nature was to Yizhak what speculation and (perhaps) astrology were to Avraham. In this light, we can comprehend why the tradition that Yizhak ordained the afternoon service *(minhah)* is derived from the verse: "And Yizhak went out to meditate in the field . . ." (Bereshit 24:63). Yizhak's place for prayer was in the field, where he could commune with nature and thus find God.[43]

---

42. Cf. Yehiel Michel Halevi Epstein, *Perush LaHaggadah shel Pesah,* p. 11.
43. Cf. P. Biberfeld, *op. cit.,* Vol. III, p. 178.

Yizhak was absorbed with the land and enriched by it materially. As the Torah records: "Yizhak sowed in that land and reaped a hundredfold the same year, and the Lord blessed him" (Bereshit 26:12). Would it be presumptuous to assert that it was his involvement with the land — agriculturally, aesthetically, and spiritually — that motivated his being charged not to leave it? Perhaps it was the love Yizhak had for nature that endeared Esav to him, for Esav was a man of the field.[44] It is in the light of Yizhak's focus on land and nature that we can understand the space allotted in the Torah to his digging of wells. And in examining some of these verses we will discover that Yizhak was not only his father's son physically, but spiritually as well.

And the Philistines sealed all the wells which his father's servants had dug in the days of his father Avraham, filling them with earth. . . . Yizhak dug anew the wells which had been dug in the days of his father Avraham . . . and he gave them the same names which his father had given them. But when Yizhak's servants, digging in the valley, found there a well of spring water, the herdsmen of Gerar quarreled with Yizhak's herdsmen . . . and when they dug another well, they disputed over that one also . . . He moved there and dug yet another well, and they did not quarrel over it . . . That night the Lord appeared to him and said, "I am the Lord God of your father Avraham. Fear not, for I am with you, and I will bless you and increase your offspring for the sake of Avraham, My servant." There he built an altar and invoked the Lord by name; there, too, he pitched his tent and Yizhak's servants started digging a well.

(Bereshit 26:15-22, 24, 25)

The Torah text raises several questions:
1. Why all the fuss by the Philistines over the wells?

---

44. Bereshit 25:27.

2. What compelled Yizhak to reopen them?
3. What is the significance of the words "which his father's servants had dug in the days of Avraham"?
4. Why did Yizhak give these wells the same names Avraham had given them?

There is obviously an association between well-digging and involvement with nature, literally and symbolically. Consideration aside that water is the catalyst through which God nurtures life, water is continuously depicted in Biblical and Rabbinic literature as a symbol of Torah. To cite but one example: "Ho, all who are thirsty come for water" (Yeshayahu 55:1). Rashi: "This refers to Torah."

As we have already pointed out, Avraham built altars and dug wells wherever he went. They were symbolic of his mission in life. He would teach ethical monotheism and preach about God; afterwards, he would build an altar or dig a well as a memorial to his work. While Avraham engaged primarily in building altars, Yizhak dug wells. Could this not have been because of his special affinity with nature?

To reinforce his teachings, Avraham gave the altars and wells names that would remind the people of God. Whenever they would pass by the altar or come to draw water at the well, they would be reminded of the lessons of Avraham. In an attempt to uproot Avraham's teachings, the Philistines sealed up the wells. When Yizhak became aware of what they had done, he reopened the wells, in order to reestablish his father's teachings.[45]

Yizhak was the true spiritual heir of Avraham, although, as we have pointed out, he had his own approach to God as well. He also had the distinct advantage of being born in the home of a righteous man — an

---

45. Cf. Y.Z. Mecklenberg, *op. cit.*, Bereshit 26:18.

advantage his father lacked — and of being given a proper spiritual upbringing from childhood. Interestingly, on the verse "And the child grew up and was weaned" (Bereshit 21:8), the Midrash states in the name of R. Hoshiah: "He was weaned from the evil inclination."[46] Apparently, Yizhak's self control began at an early age. It is no wonder that at the age of 37 he was ready to be put through the ultimate test of faith, a test his father Avraham was not ready for until the age of 137.

In God's eyes, Yizhak was indeed a special person. When a famine had broken out in the land of Canaan, God had not forbidden or prevented Avraham from going to Egypt. But when it happened again, in the time of Yizhak, the Torah records: "And there was a famine in the land — aside from the previous famine that had occurred in the days of Avraham — and Yizhak went to Avimelekh, King of the Philistines, in Gerar. The Lord had appeared to him and said, 'Do not go down to Egypt; stay in the land which I point out to you' " (Bereshit 26:1, 2). Yizhak was never to leave the chosen land of Canaan. As a sacred and unblemished human being, he was to spend his entire life in the sacred and unblemished land.[47]

We must point out that the "God through nature" philosophy, interesting and noble as it may be, does have its pitfalls: it can lead man to self-deception. One can become so enamored with the approach that he becomes blinded to all others. This point is made by Philip Biberfeld, who writes that the God through nature philosophy may very well account for Yizhak's failure to understand Yaakov, who had not followed his father's approach, but had studied with Shem and Ever. Yizhak may have doubted that Yaakov could ever achieve the

---

46. *Bereshit Rabbah* 53:14.
47. Cf. Rashi, Bereshit 26:2.

communication with the Divine that was his own experience.[48]

Rivkah, the Second Matriarch

Avraham was most cautious in selecting a wife for Yizhak. He dispatched Eliezer, his most trusted servant, instructing him: "You shall go to my country and my birthplace and take a wife for my son Yizhak" (Bereshit 24:4).

What was so special about Aram, Avraham's birthplace? Idolatry was no less prevalent there than in Canaan. What difference would it make whether Yizhak married an Aramean or a Canaanite?

In point of fact, there was no difference between the Arameans and the Canaanites regarding idolatry. It was in their approach to morality that they differed. The Canaanite women were notoriously immoral; this was not the case in Aram. While misguided theology can be corrected through proper education — a task for which Yizhak was eminently qualified — immorality is quite another matter. As such, Aram had a distinct advantage over Canaan.[49]

The conversation between Avraham and Eliezer is crucial to our understanding of the events that transpired, and we must follow it carefully. The Torah records:

> And Avraham said to the senior servant in his household, who had charge of all that he owned, "Put your hand under my thigh. And I will make you swear by the Lord, the God of heaven and the God of the earth, that you will not take a wife for my son from the daughters of the Canaanites among whom I dwell, but will go to the land of my birth and get a wife for my son Yizhak." And the servant said to him,

---

48. Cf. P. Biberfeld, *op. cit.*
49. Cf. Y.Z. Mecklenberg, *op. cit.,* Bereshit 24:4.

"What if the woman does not consent to follow me to this land? Shall I take your son back to the land from which you came?" And Avraham answered him, "On no account may you take my son back there. The Lord, the God of heaven, who took me from my father's house and from the land of my birth, who promised me under oath, saying, 'I will give this land to your offspring' — He will send His angel before you and you will get a wife for my son from there. And if the woman does not consent to follow you, you shall then be clear of this, my oath; but do not take my son back there." So the servant put his hand under the thigh of Avraham his master and swore to him as bidden.

(Bereshit 24:2-9)

Eliezer was to go to Aram and bring back the wife whom *God* had chosen for Yizhak. If she refused to go, he was to return to Canaan — free from the oath he had taken. Clearly, the selection was made by God, through an angel.

When Eliezer came to Aram, he paused and offered the following words of prayer:

O Lord, God of my master Avraham, grant me good fortune this day and deal graciously with my master Avraham. As I stand here by the spring and the daughters of the townspeople come out to draw water, let the maiden to whom I say, "Please lower your pitcher that I may drink," and who replies, "Drink, and I will also water your camels," let her be the one whom You have decreed for Your servant Yizhak. Thereby shall I know that You have dealt graciously with my master.

(Bereshit 24:12-14)

Was Eliezer's prayer an appropriate one? The Midrash is most displeased with him. Had he set up his own test? Would he have taken any woman who had offered water to him and his camels? How could he be sure that she was the one whom God had selected for Yizhak? In fact, argues the Midrash, it was God's mercy and compassion for Avraham and Yizhak that prevented the wrong woman from appearing.[50] Others feel that Eliezer sought a way by which he could identify the woman whom *God* had chosen. The sign was for himself only. He prayed that God would honor that sign and bring forth the chosen one.[51]

Whatever the meaning of Eliezer's gesture, the scheme itself would reveal personality traits in the woman that were appropriate for Yizhak's mate. A kind and understanding woman who would put personal inconvenience aside in order to help a perfect stranger, and whose sensitivities extended to the brute creation as well, would be most complementary to Yizhak, himself a man of peace and a lover of nature.

Rivkah's humility is also emphasized in the Torah. Returning with Eliezer to Canaan to become Yizhak's wife, she sees him in the distance. The Torah records: "Raising her eyes, Rivkah saw Yizhak. She dismounted from the camel and said to the servant, 'Who is that man walking in the field toward us?' And the servant said, 'That is my master.' So she took her veil and covered herself" (Bereshit 24:64, 65).

Now let us not confuse modesty with humility. To veil her face was clearly an act of modesty on Rivkah's part. To dismount the camel so that Yizhak would not have to lift his head to speak with her, while she looked down at him, showed great humility. In fact, the moment she met Yizhak she was awe-stricken — an experience she never forgot and one that affected her relationship with Yizhak for their entire married life.[52]

---

50. Cf. *Bereshit Rabbah* 60:3.
51. Cf. Naftali Zvi Yehudah Berlin, *Ha'amek Davar,* Bereshit 24:2.
52. *Ibid.,* Bereshit 24:65.

For Yizhak, it was love almost at first sight — not physical love, but a recognition of compatibility. The Torah alludes to this with the words: "The servant told Yizhak all the things that he had done. Yizhak then brought her into the tent of his mother Sarah, and he took Rivkah as his wife, and he loved her and thus found comfort after his mother's death" (Bereshit 24:66, 67). One would have expected the text to read, "He loved her and took her as his wife." The point seems to be that the love — physical attraction — came later; it was not the primary consideration in their marriage.

Another allusion to their compatibility is found in the words "And Yizhak brought her into the tent of his mother Sarah." Not until he brought her into his mother's tent, and she demonstrated that she was very much like Sarah in her righteousness, did Yizhak take her as a wife.[53]

The Incident of the Blessing

Considering Rivkah's righteousness and her great humility, the incident of Yaakov's blessing is somewhat disconcerting. Only careful analysis will reveal her motivations. When we have done so, we will be able to see her more objectively and judge her more intelligently. Perhaps then her behavior will seem less incongruous with her personality. The Torah records:

> When Yizhak was old and his eyes were too dim to see, he called his elder son Esav and said to him, "My son." He answered, "Here I am." And he said, "I am, you see, so old that I do not know how soon I may die. Take, then, your gear — your quiver and bow — and go out into the country and hunt me some game. Then make me a tasty dish

---

53. Cf. Meir Leibush Malbim, *Ha-Torah V'ha-Mizvah*, Bereshit 24:67.

such as I like, and bring it to me to eat, so that I may give you my innermost blessing before I die."

Rivkah had been listening as Yizhak spoke to his son Esav. When Esav had gone out to the country to hunt game to bring home, Rivkah said to her son Yaakov, "I overheard your father speaking to your brother Esav, saying, 'Bring me some game and make me a tasty dish to eat, that I may bless you, with the Lord's approval, before I die.' Now, my son, listen carefully as I instruct you. Go to the flock and fetch me two choice kids, and I will make of them a tasty dish for your father as he likes. Then take it to your father to eat, in order that he may bless you before he dies." Yaakov answered his mother Rivkah, "But my brother Esav is a hairy man and I am smooth-skinned. If my father touches me, I shall appear to him as a trickster and bring upon myself a curse, not a blessing." But his mother said to him, "Your curse, my son, be upon me! Just do as I say and fetch them for me."

He got them and brought them to his mother, and his mother prepared a tasty dish such as his father liked. Rivkah then took the best clothes of her elder son Esav, which were there in the house, and had her younger son Yaakov put them on; and she covered his hands and the hairless part of his neck with the skin of the kids. Then she put in the hands of her son Yaakov the tasty dish and the bread she had prepared.

He went to his father and said, "Father." And he said, "Which of my sons are you?" Yaakov said to his father, "I am Esav, your firstborn. I have done as you told me. Pray sit up and eat of my game, that you may give me your innermost blessing." Yizhak said to his son, "How did you succeed so quickly, my son?" And he said, "Because the Lord your God granted me good fortune." Yizhak said to Yaakov, "Come closer that I may feel you, my son, whether you are my son Esav or not." So Yaakov drew close to his father Yizhak, who said as he felt him, "The voice is the voice of Yaakov, but the hands are the hands of Esav." He did not recognize him because his hands were hairy, like those of his brother Esav. As he prepared to bless him, he asked, "Are you really my son Esav?" And when he said, "I am," he said, "Serve me and let me eat of my son's game that I may give you my innermost blessing." So he served him and he ate and he brought him wine and he drank. Then his father Yizhak said to him, "Come closer and kiss me, my son," and he went up and kissed him. And he smelled his clothes and he blessed him. . . .

No sooner had Yaakov left the presence of his father Yizhak — after Yizhak had finished blessing Yaakov — than his brother Esav came back from his hunt. He, too, prepared a tasty dish, and brought it to his father. And he said to his father, "Let my father sit up and eat of his son's game, so that you may give me your innermost blessing." His father Yizhak said to him, "Who are you?" And he said, "Esav, your firstborn." Yizhak was seized with violent trembling. "Who was it, then," he demanded, "that hunted game and brought it to me? Moreover, I ate of it before you came, and I blessed him; surely he must remain blessed."

(Bereshit 27:1-33)

Was this the way of a humble and righteous woman? To deceive her husband, to deprive her elder son of a blessing from his father — which by birthright he certainly deserved — and to force her younger son to be party to such a deception would seem utterly audacious, immoral, and out of character for Rivkah. Furthermore, what could she have possibly hoped to accomplish? Surely she was aware that the deception would be revealed as soon as Esav returned home from the hunt. Lastly, to bless is in God's hands, not man's. Despite her efforts, God would give the blessing to the deserving one.

Let us begin by pointing out that Rivkah knew her sons well. Like Sarah, she was able to see things objectively. But unlike Sarah, who might be accused (however unjustly) of favoring her own son over Yishmael, Rivkah had borne both sons; she loved them both. The Torah painstakingly points this out throughout the story by repeatedly referring to Esav as her elder son and Yaakov as her younger son — implying that she loved them both dearly. When Rivkah is informed that Esav plans to kill Yaakov, she instructs Yaakov to stay with Lavan, her brother, in Haran until Esav's anger subsides, and she concludes, "Let me not lose both of you in one day" (Bereshit 27:45). Here her concern for both her sons is clearly stated. As Rashi points out, she was afraid that if one killed the other the children of the deceased would rise up against the surviving brother and kill him.

Rivkah knew that Yaakov was Yizhak's true spiritual heir; he deserved the blessing. But she was a perceptive woman; she knew that Yizhak was emotionally blinded by Esav's love of nature. She had to sensitize him to the real Esav, of whom our Sages said, "He entraps his father with his words."[54] Could she confront Yizhak directly? Probably not. Rivkah was too humble with Yizhak for such a gesture. A plan had to be devised that would dramatically expose Yizhak's weakness and make him see the truth about his sons once and for all.

Rivkah knew that Yaakov deserved the blessing, but this alone would not have motivated her to act. When the children were still in her womb, it had been revealed to her that the elder would serve the younger.[55] This was her chance to bring the prophecy to fruition. Still, the plan was not so much to deceive Yizhak as it was to make him aware that he could be tricked even by his own sons. By implementing this deception, knowing full well that Yizhak would discover what had happened — indeed, because of it — Rivkah knew that Yizhak would be forced to face the truth about his sons, and thus ensure their proper place in history. For "If Yaakov, a mild man, can so easily masquerade as a skillful hunter, how much more easily can Esav masquerade as a mild man to him."[56]

---

54. Cf. Rashi, Bereshit 25:28.
55. Cf. Bereshit 25:23.
56. Cf. S.R. Hirsch, *op. cit.*, Bereshit Chapter 27.

The deception worked. Yizhak realized what had happened as soon as Esav returned. The Torah records: "Yizhak was seized with very violent trembling. 'Who was it, then, that hunted game and brought it to me? Moreover, I ate of it before you came, and I blessed him. *Surely he must remain blessed.*' " It was a gradual realization and a reconciliation as well. Mulling over in his mind what had just happened to him, he put things into proper perspective. Suddenly everything came into focus. He was not sorry for what had happened. As we read, "Surely he must remain blessed."

Recognizing her noble attempt and his feeble judgment, Yizhak does not reproach Rivkah for her impropriety, or even mention it to her. But to Esav he remarks, "Your brother came in guile and took your blessing" (Bereshit 27:35). When a deception occurs, however noble it may be, its unethical component must be recognized.

To further emphasize Rivkah's nobility, the incident of the blessing is concluded with a comment by the Torah itself. We read: "And Yizhak sent Yaakov off to Padan Aram — to Lavan, the son of Bethuel the Aramite, the brother of Rivkah, who was the mother of Yaakov and Esav" (Bereshit 28:5). The last phrase is clearly redundant. There is no need to identify Rivkah as the mother of Yaakov and Esav — not after all that has happened. Even Rashi is surprised, and comments: "I don't know what this phrase has to teach us." Would it be too presumptuous to suggest that the Torah is not merely identifying Rivkah as the mother of the two sons, but pointing out that despite all that had happened — that she was forced to engineer a deception, that Esav now threatened Yaakov's life, and that she was compelled to send Yaakov away — she still loved both her sons? Is this phrase not the Torah's own approbation of her behavior? Indeed, Rivkah was the mother of Yaakov *and* Esav.

Chapter 3

Yaakov, Rahel, and Leah

The life of Yaakov, whom some of our Sages consider the foremost of the patriarchs, is depicted in the Torah as virtually an endless period of difficulty and travail, moving from one crisis to another and from one tragedy to another. How symbolic of the history of the Jewish people, his namesake, from its beginning until present times. How intriguing is the remark in the Midrash that Avraham was saved from the fiery furnace mainly because God foresaw that Yaakov would descend from him.[57]

Yaakov and Esav, as depicted in the Torah, symbolize the endless struggle between good and evil, Israel and the nations, Torah and paganism. It seems that the struggle began, at least symbolically, right in the womb. As the Torah records:

> Yizhak pleaded with the Lord on behalf of his wife because she was barren, and the Lord responded to his plea, and his wife Rivkah conceived. But the children struggled in her womb, and she said, "If so, why do I exist?" She went to inquire of the Lord. And the Lord answered her, "Two nations are in your womb, two people apart while still in your body; one people shall be mightier than the other, and the elder shall serve the younger."
>
> (Bereshit 25:21-23)

---

57. Cf. *Bereshit Rabbah* 63:2.

Even at birth, Yaakov held the heel of Esav, and he was so named to continuously bring home the message that the elder of the two would serve the younger. We have already pointed out its significance with regard to the blessing. The Midrash goes even further in identifying the struggle, commenting: "Whenever Rivkah passed the school of Shem and Ever, Yaakov would move convulsively in his efforts to be born; when she passed the gates of a pagan temple, Esav would do so."[58] The symbolism continued into birth, where the Torah records:

> The first one emerged red, like a hairy mantle all over, so they named him Esav. Then his brother emerged, holding onto the heel of Esav, so they named him Yaakov. And the boys grew up. Esav became a skillful hunter, a man of the fields, but Yaakov was a mild man who stayed in camp.
>
> (Bereshit 25:25-27)

Who was destined to inherit the spiritual calling of Avraham and Yizhak? In the very process of birth, the Torah alludes to the posture that would be assumed by Yaakov to attain what he rightfully deserved: the birthright and the blessing. For just as the name "Yaakov" derives from *akov,* meaning "to come from behind," and as such to do the unexpected, so was Yaakov the man destined to attain his goals through means that were out of the ordinary and completely atypical of his personality.[59]

Both children were given the same love and the same attention. Perhaps this was the mistake! Children should be treated as individuals, each according to his own strengths and weaknesses.[60] This point is

---

58. *Ibid.,* 63:6.
59. Cf. S.R. Hirsch, *op. cit.,* Bereshit 22:18, 25:26.
60. *Ibid.,* Bereshit 25:27.

made quite succinctly in the Book of Proverbs: "Train a lad in the way he should go; he will not swerve from it even in old age" (Mishle 22:6). Each child must be individually trained and continuously monitored if we are to achieve the desired lifelong result of righteousness and commitment. Our contention is further confirmed by the comment of Rashi: "When they were children, their character was not detected from their behavior. But when they reached the age of thirteen, one went to study while the other practiced idolatry."[61]

Despite the potential and the promise Yaakov had shown even at an early age, the Torah records: "Yizhak favored Esav because he had a taste for game, but Rivkah loved Yaakov" (Bereshit 25:28). Perhaps it was Esav's great strength and courage that Yizhak admired; perhaps it was his love of nature, as was already indicated. Perhaps it was simply his love of the outdoors and the hunt, as the Torah indicates. How interesting that the Torah finds no need to justify Rivkah's feelings. It was not merely a particular attribute that endeared Yaakov to her; it was his whole personality.

Perhaps there was an additional reason why Rivkah gave Yaakov a special measure of love and affection — one to which only a mother would be sensitive. Rivkah knew that Yaakov, Yizhak's true spiritual heir, deserved a great deal more love than had been shown him by his father. Seeing his disappointment, she tried to compensate with a greater measure of her own love. The lesson is indeed relevant in every generation.

The first direct indication of the conflict between Yaakov and Esav is the incident of the selling of the birthright. It must be read and studied carefully in order to avoid misinterpretation. We read as follows:

---

61. Rashi, Bereshit 25:26.

Once, when Yaakov was cooking a stew, Esav came in from the outdoors, famished. And Esav said to Yaakov, "Give me some of that red stuff to gulp down, for I am famished," which is why he was named Edom. Yaakov said, "Sell me your birthright." And Esav said, "I am at the point of death, so of what use is my birthright to me?" Yaakov said, "Swear to me." So he swore to him, and sold his birthright to Yaakov. *And Yaakov gave Esav bread and lentil stew.* And he ate, drank, rose, and went his way. Thus did Esav spurn the birthright.   (Bereshit 25:29-34)

A simple reading of the text would lead us to conclude that Yaakov's behavior toward his brother Esav was insensitive at best, and immoral at worst. In light of what we have thus far said about Yaakov, however, such a conclusion would be incongruous. In fact, to assume that Yaakov took advantage of Esav's weakened condition to gain the birthright is simply indefensible. A little understanding of Biblical Hebrew will prevent us from making a hasty judgment, and at the same time restore our confidence in Yaakov's integrity.

It can be established from the Torah text that Yaakov gave Esav his food before any discussion of the birthright had begun. The key words are: "And Yaakov gave Esav bread and lentil stew." In Biblical Hebrew, when the conversive "vav" is used, the word order is usually "verb, noun." But there are times when the "vav" is attached to the noun rather than the verb, and the word order is "noun, verb." The former is called *Avar ha-Mesudar;* the latter, *Avar ha-Mukdam.* When the former is used, the events in the story are sequential; in the latter cases, the change in form is to teach us that the event in the verse occurred earlier. The verse above is an example of *Avar ha-Mukdam* and an indication to the reader that the giving of the food took place earlier. It should read, in translation, "And Yaakov had given Esav bread and lentil stew."

What happened was as follows: Esav came home from the hunt, hungry and tired. He asked Yaakov for some of the food he was preparing, and was given it. Then a discussion ensued regarding the birthright. Esav was not at all interested in the birthright, and he told this to Yaakov. Yaakov, on the other hand, was most interested, for it meant that he would be the spiritual heir to their father Yizhak. To confirm Esav's disinterest in the birthright, Yaakov had him swear. The story ends with an affirmation from the Torah itself that Esav was disinterested: "Thus did Esav spurn the birthright."[62]

Yaakov, having acquired both the birthright and the blessing, incurred the wrath of his brother to such an extent that Esav betrayed his true self as a "man of the hunt." As the Torah records, "Esav harbored a grudge against Yaakov because of the blessing which his father had given him, and Esav said to himself, 'Let but the mourning period of my father come, and I will kill my brother Yaakov' " (Bereshit 27:41).

Following his mother's instructions, Yaakov leaves Canaan and journeys to Haran, to the home of Lavan, his uncle. Like Avraham, his grandfather, Yaakov also must have been beset by fear and loneliness when he left home to journey to a place of which he knew virtually nothing. And in a sense, he also experienced the trial of his father Yizhak. For Yaakov's life was threatened — not only by Esav, but by heavenly angels as well. It happened in a dream Yaakov had, depicted in the Torah as follows:

> Yaakov left Be'er Sheva and set out for Haran. He came upon *the place* and stopped there for the night, for the sun had set. Taking one of the stones of *the place,* he put it under his head and lay down in *the*

---

62. Cf. Y.Z. Mecklenberg, *op. cit.,* Bereshit 25:34, also Ramban *ad loc.*

place. He had a dream; a ladder was set on the ground and its top reached to the sky, and angels of God were going up and down on it. And the Lord suddenly was standing beside him and said, "I am the Lord, the God of your father Avraham and the God of Yizhak: the ground on which you are lying I will give to you and your offspring. Your descendants shall be as the dust of the earth; you shall spread out to the west and to the east, to the north and to the south. All the families of the earth shall bless themselves by you and your descendants. Remember, I am with you: I will protect you wherever you go and will bring you back to this land. I will not leave you until I have done what I have promised you."

(Bereshit 28:10-15)

Strangely, we are not told where Yaakov rested on this first lonely night of his journey. It is referred to simply as "the place." Indeed, this term is mentioned three times in verse 11. Yaakov came upon *the place,* took some stones from *the place,* and rested in *the place.* Why the redundancy? It was obviously a place of importance, clearly indicated by the use of the definite article. But where was it?

There is one other instance in the Torah where the word is used. When Avraham brought Yizhak as a sacrifice, he was told to go to the land of Moriah. After a three-day journey, the Torah records, "And they arrived at the place of which God had told him" (Bereshit 22:9). It is Moriah which is here referred to as *the place* three times. Rashi makes the point of identification quite clearly: "The Scripture does not mention which place, but by writing *the place,* it refers to the place mentioned already in another passage: Mount Moriah."[63]

Yaakov rested at Moriah, where his father Yizhak had been brought as an offering. Some commentators go as far as to say that *the place* refers to the altar upon which Yizhak was brought. As such, Yaakov

---

63. Rashi, Bereshit 28:11.

lay down and rested on the very altar upon which Yizhak had been placed, though he was unaware of it at the time.[64]

The Midrash comments: Yaakov's life was threatened at that moment by the angels. In heaven they saw him as the embodiment of the noblest human potentials; when they descended the ladder to the earth and saw him sleeping — exhibiting human frailties and limitations — they were angered and began to mock him. Suddenly, says the Torah, the Lord appeared beside him and saved his life.[65] Indeed, the Midrash makes the parallelism to the experience of Yizhak at Moriah that much more complete.

The dream of the ladder was addressed to Yaakov in terms of three facets of his life: as the son of Yizhak, as the third patriarch, and as the quintessential human being. In the first instance, it meant the following:

It was God's will that providence be manifest upon Avraham and his seed to a greater measure than upon any other human beings. Avraham's seed would inherit the Holy Land and they would be greatly multiplied upon the earth. These promises were also made to Yizhak. Now they were being made to Yaakov.

The ladder that stood upon the earth and reached to heaven represented the Temple, to be built on that spot, from which the Divine influence would be manifested upon all of Israel. The ascending and descending angels were those that handled the sacrifices brought by the people of Israel in the Temple. Bearing the sacrifices, they would rise to heaven and then return to earth to redeem Israel. The appearance of the Lord beside Yaakov symbolized the special measure of Divine providence granted to the Jewish people.

---

64. Cf. E. Ashkenazi, *op. cit.,* Ma'ase Avot Bereshit 28:11.
65. Cf. *Bereshit Rabbah* 68:18.

The second promise — the inheritance of the land — was repeated to Yaakov with the words "the ground on which you are lying I will give to you and your offspring." Lastly, the promise that the nation of Israel would be greatly multiplied was repeated to him with the words "Your descendants shall be as the dust of the earth." For Yaakov this was the fulfillment of a Divine promise that would commence in his lifetime.

Yaakov was also addressed as the nation of Israel, for he was its third patriarch. He was told of its future among the nations of the world. The Midrash spells this out quite succinctly:

> Said R. Shmuel, son of Nahman: "The words 'And behold, angels ascending and descending' refer to the guardian angels of the nations . . . For the Holy One Blessed Be He showed our father Yaakov the guardian angel of Babylonia rise seventy steps and then descend, the guardian angel of Media rise fifty steps and then descend, the guardian angel of Greece rise one hundred steps and then descend, the guardian angel of Rome (Edom) rise but he knew not how many. At that moment, Yaakov began to tremble and said, 'Perhaps this one will never fall?' Said the Holy One Blessed Be He to him, 'Have no fear, Yaakov my servant . . . even if you were to see him rise and sit by My side, I would cause him to fall from there.' "
>
> (Midrash Tanhuma: VaYeze 2)

God revealed to Yaakov that the nations of the world would rise and fall in their struggle for power, one after the other. Even Edom, which according to tradition represents Rome at first and Christianity later, will eventually fall. God's sudden appearance beside Yaakov indicated that the nation of Israel would be worthy of special providence that would guarantee it eternity.

Lastly, the dream was addressed to Yaakov as the quintessential human being. In this regard, a remark by the Midrash is noteworthy:

"Israel will in the future go to Avraham and say, 'Teach us the Torah,' and he will respond, 'Go to Yizhak, who learned more than I.' And Yizhak in turn will say, 'Go to Yaakov, who ministered more than I.' "[66] It is evident that the Midrash regards Yaakov as superior to both his father and his grandfather in some ways.[67] Perhaps it was some of his life experiences that exposed him to aspects of the Divine that the others had not known, but it was also the medium through which he came to God that made a difference.

Unlike Avraham, whose perception of God began with speculation, Yaakov derived his knowledge of God from prophecy. The dream of the ladder is an outstanding example.[68] In fact, that which man is capable of perceiving through an encounter with the Divine can never be acquired through speculation alone. There is a qualitative difference between the two. Speculation is a cognitive gesture that involves man alone; prophecy, both cognitive and sensuous, is an encounter between man and God.

Whatever the significance of the dream — whether to reiterate the principle of providence, to establish the chosenness of the land of Israel, or, as Nahmanides posits, to teach that all God's deeds in this world are actualized through angels, who continuously return to Him for direction — it was addressed to Yaakov as the quintessential human being, who had achieved near-perfection of his spiritual potential.

Yaakov was more than impressed with the dream; he was spellbound. We read: "And Yaakov carried his feet and came to the land of the Easterners" (Bereshit 29:1). Two interpretations are given by the Sages:

---

66. *Shemot Rabbah* 2:12.
67. Cf. S.R. Hirsch, *op. cit.,* Bereshit 28:13.
68. Cf. *Bereshit Rabbah* 69:1, also Y. Arama, *op. cit.,* VaYeze, p. 190.

1. Normally one is carried by his feet. This one carries his feet? It was because he cleaved to the place and didn't want to turn away. With great difficulty, he forced himself to go. He literally "carried his feet."[69]
2. Yaakov lifted his feet out of great joy. He went happily on his journey because God had promised to be with him wherever he would go.[70]

High in hopes and with great joy, Yaakov encounters some shepherds at a well outside the city of his destination. At last he sees some people with whom he can communicate. He speaks. But from the conversation that ensues, it seems that the shepherds were not at all as anxious as he to converse. The Torah records:

> Yaakov said to them, "My friends, where are you from?" And they said, "We are from Haran." He said to them, "Do you know Lavan, the son of Nahor?" And they said, "Yes, we do." He continued, "Is he well?" They answered, "He is; and there is his daughter Rahel coming with the flock."
>
> (Bereshit: 29:4-6)

Why so cold a reaction from the shepherds? Was it because he was a stranger? Perhaps so. The Midrash notes the problem and comments: "And they said, 'He is well, and if it is conversation you want, his daughter is coming with the flock. Speak with her, for women are babblers.' "[71]

Yaakov, the new man, with renewed strength and courage, doesn't react; he pursues the matter at hand as if he had been welcomed. It must

---

69. *Midrash Ohr Afelah,* Bereshit 29:1.
70. Cf. *Midrash Aggadah* 29:1.
71. *Bereshit Rabbah* 70:10.

have been his renewed strength that enabled him to lift the stone over the well single-handedly — a task that had usually been done by all the shepherds together.[72]

Yaakov's need for communication was not resolved until he met Lavan. As the Torah records, "And he (Lavan) brought him into his house, and he (Yaakov) told him all these things" (Bereshit 29:13). Yaakov unburdened his heart. He told Lavan of his hardships and his poverty. Like a devoted member of the family, Lavan offered a listening ear. Little did Yaakov know at the time that his suffering was far from over. Little did he know that it would be more than twenty years before he would return home with family and substance. Little did he know that these years would be marked by frustration and disappointment, all the while enriching his faith and convictions. Indeed, those years were like a fiery furnace that consumed the weak but tempered the strong.

What were some of Yaakov's outstanding virtues?

Perseverance in times of stress was perhaps his most identifying characteristic. His ability to face and handle the disappointments and tragedies he suffered in life without losing either courage or ambition betrays a man of unusual dedication and great fortitude. This attribute is alluded to at his birth, where we read that he was "holding onto the heel of Esav." It manifests itself particularly in the birthright and blessing incidents, but also in the journey to Haran, the years of labor to win the hand of Rahel, the journey home, and the encounter with Esav. These events were all conducive to surrender, but Yaakov persevered. Again, how analagous is his life to the history of the nation of Israel.

Patience and self-control were also among his virtues. He was

---

72. Ramban, Bereshit 29:2.

unprovoked by the scheming Lavan, the violation of Dinah, or the painful and incriminating dreams of his beloved son Yosef. Even toward the end of his life, when he was informed that Yosef was alive, he was not provoked to anger against his other sons for their horrendous deed.

In only two instances do we read that "Yaakov became very angry." They have a common denominator: both concern fundamental principles of the Torah. The first incident is recorded as follows:

> When Rahel saw that she had borne Yaakov no children, she became envious of her sister; and Rahel said to Yaakov, "Give me children or I shall die." And Yaakov became angry with Rahel and said, "Can I take the place of God, who has denied you fruit of the womb?"
> (Bereshit 30:1, 2)

What was it that made Yaakov, the man of peace, patience, and perseverance, so insensitive to the pain of his beloved Rahel? It was her magical thinking. Rahel implied that Yaakov had merely to pray and his wishes would be granted. Man orders and God complies. This was convoluted thinking, and it had no place in Yaakov's life. Rahel had to be disciplined most emphatically. There is a time for love and there is a time not to be loving. In the same vein, Ramban explains:

> Rahel asked Yaakov that he give her children, but her intent was truly to say that he should pray on her behalf and continue, indeed, to pray, until God would . . . grant her children. If not, she would mortify herself out of grief. In her envy, she spoke improperly, thinking that because Yaakov loved her he would fast, put on sackcloth with ashes, and pray until she would be granted children, so that she should not die of her grief. It is not in the power of the righteous that their prayer be heard and answered in every case, and because she spoke in the manner of yearning women who are loved,

thus attempting to frighten him with her death, his anger was kindled.[73]

In desperation, Rahel had resorted to primitive thinking. False notions about providence that lead to inappropriate behavior are certainly good reason to be concerned, and valid motivation for constructive criticism. This is what was behind Yaakov's harsh words.

The second incident concerns Lavan. When Yaakov and his family were preparing to leave Haran and journey to Canaan, Rahel took her father's house gods and hid them among her belongings. It was a move she hoped would wean her father from idol worship.[74] When Lavan discovered that the idols were missing, he pursued Yaakov and accused him of stealing them. We read:

> "Very well, you had to leave because you were longing for your father's house; but why did you steal my gods?" Yaakov answered Lavan, saying, "Anyone with whom you find your gods shall not remain alive! In the presence of our kinsmen, point out what I have of yours and take it." Yaakov, of course, did not know that Rahel had appropriated them.
>
> (Bereshit 31:30-32)

Lavan searched their persons and their belongings, but found nothing. We read, "Yaakov became angry and took up his grievance with Lavan" (Bereshit 31:36). The bravado with which Yaakov spoke had already indicated his repressed anger, but now it surfaced. To be accused of theft by a thief, by one who himself had engaged in all sorts of trickery and subterfuge, was simply too much for Yaakov to quietly

---

73. *Ibid.,* Bereshit 30:1.
74. Cf. Rashi, Bereshit 31:19.

endure. Indeed, the false accusation of a righteous man is sufficient cause for anger. We must take note here of Yaakov's words, for they betray the resentment and utter frustration that had built up in his mind through the twenty years he spent in Haran. The Torah records:

These twenty years I have spent in your service, your ewes and your she-goats never miscarried; nor did I feast on rams from your flock. That which was torn by beasts I never brought to you. I myself made good the loss; you exacted it of me — whether snatched by day or snatched by night; and sleep fled from my eyes. Of the twenty years that I spent in your household, I served you fourteen years for your two daughters and six years for your flocks, and you changed my wages time and time again. Had not the God of my father — the God of Avraham and the Fear of Yizhak — been with me, you would have sent me away empty-handed. But God took notice of my plight and the toil of my hands, and He rendered judgment last night.

(Bereshit 31:38-42)

Can we believe our eyes? Is this the real Yaakov speaking? Is this the man of patience and kindness, the master of self-control? Indeed, the bubble did finally burst.[75]

Rahel and Leah

What is revealed in the Torah about Rahel and Leah, the last of the matriarchs, is limited to their childbearing years, and focuses on their strong desire to be the mothers of the nation of Israel. We must keep this point in mind while assessing their behavior.

One might suggest that, in personality, Rahel resembled Sarah,

---

75. Cf. Benno Jacob, *Commentary on Genesis,* trans. I. Jacob (New York, 1974), 31:38.

while Leah resembled Rivkah. Rahel was strong-willed and forceful, enabling her to confront Yaakov with the words "Give me children." In point of fact, it was not only her words; her actions paralleled Sarah's actions. When Rahel saw that she had no children, she said to Yaakov, "Here is my maid Bilhah. Consort with her, that she may bear on my knees and that through her I, too, may have children" (Bereshit 30:3).

Nevertheless, there was an important difference in their motivation. While Sarah hoped to gain favor in God's eyes through this gesture and be blessed with a child of her own in reward, Rahel had no such hopes. She would have been satisfied merely to bear the responsibility of raising Bilhah's child in the traditions of Yaakov. In light of the fact that God had promised Avraham that he would have a child through Sarah, while no such promise had been made to Yaakov and Rahel, this is quite understandable.[76]

Leah's personality was closer to that of Rivkah. She was humble and passive. It seems that she was able to contain her hurt and embarrassment quite well, for when the Torah introduces her we are told, "And Leah's eyes were weak." The Talmud comments: "She wept because she thought she was destined to marry Esav" (Bava Batra 123a). The Midrash adds: "For people said, 'So has it been arranged: the elder will be given to the elder and the younger to the younger.' And she wept and said, 'Let it be God's will that I do not fall to the lot of the wicked.' "[77]

Although Leah was happy that she had not been given to Esav, she must surely have been saddened when she was forced upon Yaakov. She must have sensed from the beginning that her life with him would be strained at best, that she would only see happiness if she would bear

---

76. Cf. N.Z.Y. Berlin, *op. cit.,* Bereshit 30:2.
77. *Bereshit Rabbah* 70:15.

him children. These feelings come clearly into focus in the naming of her children. The Torah records:

> Leah conceived and bore a son, and named him Reuven, for she declared, "It means: 'The Lord has seen my affliction'; it also means: 'Now my husband will love me.' " She conceived again and bore a son, and declared, "This is because the Lord heard that I was unloved, and has given me this one also"; so she named him Shimon. Again she conceived and bore a son, and declared, "This time my husband will become attached to me, for I have given him three sons." Therefore, he was named Levi. She conceived again and bore a son, and declared, "This time I will praise the Lord." Therefore, she named him Yehudah. Then she stopped bearing.
>
> (Bereshit 29:32-35)

Each time, Leah connected the birth of the child with God's name *Hashem,* which symbolizes the attribute of mercy. It is quite obvious here that she was preoccupied with her marital relationship. But it also attests to the good feeling she had about herself with the birth of each child, and her strong belief that her relationship with Yaakov was improving.

What was the relationship of the two sisters to each other?

Until they were married, and probably for some time hence, Leah and Rahel were very close. One illustration will make this sufficiently clear. On the night of Yaakov's marriage, Lavan substituted Leah for Rahel. The Torah records, "When morning came, there was Leah!" How was it possible that Yaakov was unaware of this substitution? The Sages explain:

> In the morning there was Leah, but in the evening it was not Leah, for Yaakov had given Rahel personal signs, things that they alone knew amongst themselves (perhaps to avoid such a problem). When Rahel

saw that Leah was being brought to Yaakov instead of her, she thought, "Now my sister will be shamed." She, therefore, revealed those personal signs to Leah.

(Rashi: Bereshit 29:25)

This expression of unbounded love and compassion was so favored by God that it was responsible, to some extent, for the survival of Israel. The point is made in the Midrash. When the Jewish people were exiled from the land of Israel, the patriarchs and the prophets appealed to the Almighty, pleading with Him to return the exiles to the land and restore the kingdom. But they were unsuccessful. Then Rahel stepped forth with the words:

> Master of the universe! It is well known to You that Yaakov Your servant loved me deeply and worked seven years for my father to wed me. When the seven years passed and the time came for me to be married to him, my father planned to substitute my sister for me. I became aware of the plan, and it disturbed me greatly. I informed my husband and gave him a sign, so that he could differentiate between my sister and myself, and my father couldn't exchange us. Afterwards, I regretted what I had done and contained my yearning, and had pity on my sister so that she would not be shamed. In the evening, they substituted my sister for me, but I revealed to her all the signs that I had given to my husband, so that he would think it was I. This was not all. I hid under the bed in which he lay with my sister. He spoke with her and she was still. I answered him regarding everything, so that he would not recognize my sister's voice. I acted righteously with her. I didn't envy her, nor allow her to be shamed.[78]

It was this act of kindness and self-denial — an act somewhat similar to what Sarah had done with Hagar for Avraham's sake — that moved

---

78. Introduction to *Ekhah Rabbatti* 23.

God to act with compassion toward the people of Israel; He promised to redeem them and restore them to the land. In the words of the Midrash: "For you, Rahel," said the Lord, "I will restore Israel to their place."

But Rahel was only human; she had human feelings and human weaknesses. After the birth of several children to Leah, we read, "And Rahel saw that she did not give birth, and she envied her sister" (Bereshit 30:1). How strangely reminiscent of Sarah! The friction between Rahel and Leah, which continued through their childbearing years, is seen with the naming of the second child of Bilhah, Rahel's maid. "Powerful wrestlings have I wrestled with my sister," said Rahel, "but I finally prevailed" (Bereshit 30:8).

How stress and competition change friend to foe! Kindness and devotion gave way to irrational thinking and arrogance toward Yaakov, as Rahel turns to him, saying, "Give me children or I shall die."

There is an interesting conversation between Rahel and Leah that many have tended to misinterpret. It concerns flowers. The text reads:

> Once, at the time of the wheat harvest, Reuven came upon some *duda'im* in the field and brought them to his mother Leah. Rahel said to Leah, "Please give me some of your son's *duda'im.*" But she said to her, "Was it not enough for you to take away my husband, that you would also take my son's *duda'im?*" Rahel replied, "Then let him lie with you tonight in return for your son's *duda'im.*" When Yaakov came home from the field that evening, Leah went out to meet him and said, "You are to sleep with me, for I have hired you with my son's *duda'im.*" And he lay with her that night.
>
> (Bereshit 30:14-17)

Several questions arise from this rather strange story:
1. What are *duda'im* and what is their nature?

2. Why did Reuven bring them to his mother?
3. Why did Rahel want them?
4. What is the significance of Leah's response?
5. Exactly what did Rahel agree to in exchange for the *duda'im?*

There is a difference of opinion in the Talmud on the identification of this flower. One opinion says it was the mandrake; another, that it was the violet. A third opinion says that it was the mandrake flower in contradistinction from its roots.[79] The Talmud also states that at the time mandrakes were commonly believed to be an aphrodisiac. If the flowers were violets (Rashi: Jasmin), their aroma could likewise have been known to stimulate sexual desire.

Reuven was about four years of age at the time. It is difficult to conceive that he had anything in mind other than expressing his love to his mother. The point made by Malbim — Reuven was aware of the power of the mandrake flower, and his mother's desire to endear herself to Yaakov by giving him as many children as possible — is somewhat difficult to accept.[80]

Whatever the motivation of Reuven, Rahel wanted the *duda'im* because they were beautiful and aromatic. According to Nahmanides, this was her only motivation. She knew that her salvation would only come through prayer; magic and incantations were not her way. The proof, says Nahmanides, is that Reuven brought his mother the branches or the fruit of the *duda'im,* rather than the stem (root). It was the latter that was claimed to be effective in inducing conception. Others disagree with this approach, however.[81]

---

79. Sanhedrin 99b.
80. Cf. M.L. Malbim, *op. cit.,* Bereshit 30:14.
81. Cf. Ramban, Bereshit 30:14. Comp. Hayyim ben Atar, *Ohr ha-Hayyim,* Bereshit 30:15.

It could be contended that the whole conversation between Rahel and Leah on this matter was innocent teasing and jesting. Let us recall Leah's words: "Was it not enough for you to take away my husband, that you also take my son's *duda'im?*" The comparison of Yaakov to a few flowers or even the mere juxtaposition of the two could never have been meant to be taken seriously.[82]

Lastly, Rahel agrees to allow Leah to have Yaakov that night. Despite what we have just said about their conversation, the decision here was a serious one. But it was out of line. It is no wonder that Rashi comments: "Because she had thought lightly of cohabiting with so righteous a man, she was not privileged to be buried with him" (Bereshit 30:15).

Rahel's prayers were finally answered. Leah had three more children. Then the Torah records: "And God remembered Rahel; God heeded her and opened her womb. She conceived and bore a son, and said, 'God has taken away my disgrace.' So she named him Yosef, which is to say, 'May the Lord add another son for me' " (Bereshit 30:22-24). Regardless of the significance of the *duda'im,* Leah did not rely on them. She prayed for more children and God answered her.[83] Whatever Rahel may have had in mind with the *duda'im,* she subsequently prayed to God for children as well and, as we see, she too was answered.[84]

The Torah has made it sufficiently clear to us, in the naming of the children and in the *duda'im* incident, that an uncompromising rivalry existed between the two sisters that may very well have persisted until

---

82. Cf. S.R. Hirsch, *op. cit.,* Bereshit 30:14.
83. Cf. M.L. Malbim, *op. cit.,* Bereshit 30:17.
84. *Ibid.,* 30:22.

their motherhood roles were virtually over. The tension relaxed at that point, they were able to live together in peace. Their former affection and devotion to one another was restored, so that when the time came for them to leave Haran, they were in complete agreement. When Yaakov called for them to ask their advice on his plan to return to Canaan, the Torah states: "And Rahel and Leah answered him, '. . . whatever God has told you to do, do it' " (Bereshit 31:14, 16). They were of one heart and spoke with one voice.

Wrestling With the Angel

Yaakov had spent twenty years in Haran acquiring and raising a family, and securing his material needs. The time had come to return to Canaan, the land of his forefathers, the land that had been promised to his seed. At one point in the journey, Yaakov brought his family and belongings aross the Yabbok River, and he himself returned to the other side, where he remained alone through the night. The Torah records a most interesting phenomenon:

> Yaakov was left alone. And a man wrestled with him until the break of dawn. When he saw that he had not prevailed against him, he wrenched Yaakov's hip at its socket, so that the socket of his hip was strained as he wrestled with him. Then he said, "Let me go, for dawn is breaking." But he answered, "I will not let you go unless you bless me." Said the other, "What is your name?" He replied, "Yaakov." Said he, "Your name shall no longer be Yaakov, but Yisrael, for you have struggled with beings Divine and human, and have prevailed."
> (Bereshit 32:25-29)

Several questions arise from this event:
1. Why did Yaakov remain alone on the other side of the Yabbok?

2. Who was the man with whom he strove?
3. What is the significance of their conversation?

Our Sages tell us that Yaakov had returned to the other side of the Yabbok River to get some small utensils he had forgotten there.[85] He remained there alone for the night because there was probably insufficient time to return before nightfall. Now, why would he have returned for some small utensils? Interestingly, the Talmud comments: "From here we learn that to the righteous their money is dearer than their body. And why is this so? Because they do not stretch out their hands to robbery."[86]

The Talmud is teaching us that that which a person acquires honestly becomes very precious to him. Yaakov had worked very hard to acquire his wealth. He didn't consider any of his possessions trivial. Quite the contrary. Wastefulness is sinful.[87]

A dramatically different approach is taken by the renowned 17th century commentator Shlomo Efrayim Linchitz, in his work *Kli Yekar.*

Yaakov's concern for material things, to the point where he put his life in danger by returning acrosss the Yabbok to pick up some small utensils, indicates a change in his thinking. He had become a wealthy man, and consequently was a prime target for the evil inclination — the drive within every human being for gratification and acquisition, which knows no bounds. This was the *man* with whom Yaakov strove.

There is something unique about the evil inclination: it never comes uninvited. When a man gives in to his desires — whether for power,

---

85. Hullin 91a.
86. *Ibid.*
87. Cf. S.R. Hirsch, *op. cit.,* Bereshit 30:25.

physical gratification, or material acquisition — he opens the door for the evil inclination within him to take control. He has merely to compromise on one seemingly insignificant point, and the precedent is set for the future. This was the case with Yaakov. Once he put his life in danger by crossing the Yabbok merely to pick up small utensils, his control had been relaxed. He had become too concerned with material things, and his evil inclination began to wrestle, so to speak, with his essence, i.e., his pure soul.

The words "until the break of dawn" allude to the notion that the coming of daylight, literally and symbolically, had a profound effect upon Yaakov. He had struggled with his evil inclination all night. But when the sun rose in the morning he "saw the light" in every sense of the term. The coming of day reinforced his belief in God the Creator, who rolls away light before darkness and darkness before light, who causes the day to pass and the night to come, the night to pass and the day to come. Yaakov's commitment was strengthened and his control over his evil inclination was rejuvenated. Further, all things in his life were again seen in their proper perspective.[88]

But there is still more that this brief incident in Yaakov's life brings to mind. Perhaps he crossed the Yabbok again because he needed to be alone to think out his life — its past, its present, and its future. He had been told that his brother Esav was coming to meet him with a powerful force of men. Once more he would be faced with imminent danger, and this frightened him. Alone, in the quiet of the night, he must have recollected the past. The *birthright* and the *blessing:* Was it all worthwhile? Even more importantly, was it in accordance with God's will? Were he to live his life over, would he make the same decisions?

---

88. Cf. Shlomo Efrayim Linchitz, *Kli Yekar,* Bereshit 32:25.

Perhaps this was the *angel* with which he struggled all night. Does not the Talmud teach: "Satan, the evil inclination, and the Angel of Death are all one"?[89] Only after such thorough introspection was Yaakov able to pursue the journey home, confident and self-assured.

Quite confirming of our approach here is the naming of the place. We read: "So Yaakov named the place Peniel, meaning, 'I have seen a Divine being face to face, yet my life has been preserved' " (Bereshit 32:31). He wrestled with the reality of his existence — symbolically depicted as the angel — all through the night, but by morning everything was resolved. His life, his essence, his integrity as a man created in the image of God and as the third of the patriarchs, had been preserved in his mind. He bore no guilt concerning the past, accepted the present, and proceeded confidently to the future. This is made clear in the name given to him by the angel: "Your name shall no longer be Yaakov but Yisrael, for you have striven with beings Divine and human and you have prevailed." The true *you* has prevailed.

Unfortunately, the tragedy of Yaakov's life did not end here. The Torah records the violation of Dinah by the men of Shechem, the discontentment of the brothers with Yosef, and the tragic consequences that were brought upon the family — all of which must have had a profound effect upon Yaakov's well-being and peace of mind. Indeed, according to our Sages, from the day he was told that Yosef had been killed till the day it was revealed to him that he still lived, the spirit of prophecy left Yaakov. This is confirmed in the Torah.[90]

Yosef sends for his father, and Yaakov and the family go down to Egypt. Proudly, Yosef brings his father to Pharaoh, and a brief but unique conversation takes place. We read:

---

89. Bava Batra 16a.
90. Cf. Rashi, Bereshit 45:27.

Pharaoh asked Yaakov, "How many are the days of the years of your life?" And Yaakov answered Pharaoh, "The days of the years of my sojourn are one hundred and thirty years. Few and hard have been the days of the years of my life, and they do not come up to the days of the years of the lives of my fathers during their sojourns." Then Yaakov bade Pharaoh farewell, and he left Pharaoh's presence.

(Bereshit 47:7-10)

The great sage encounters the great monarch. Of different cultures and commitment, for sure, but they are both men of experience who have lived full lives. This they share. Man's ultimate concern and question in life is "meaning." What is the meaning of life, and how much of one's life was spent in a meaningful way? In the end, this is all that matters. As such, Pharaoh asks Yaakov, "How many days of your life would you consider to have been good days: days of accomplishment and true happiness?" And Yaakov answers, "Not many, not nearly as many as the days in the lives of my fathers."[91]

Yaakov agrees with Pharaoh that it is not the quantity of years that makes for a good life, but their quality. However, there is more. By referring to life as a sojourn, a fleeting shadow, he implies that there is an existence after the one in this world, i.e., an afterlife.[92] Perhaps he is alluding to the fact that those like himself who, despite their righteousness, lived tragic lives barely interspersed with moments of true happiness, will be amply rewarded in the next world. Indeed, the principle of an afterlife, perhaps first alluded to by Yaakov, has been a fundamental principle of the Jewish religion for all time.

Yaakov lived out his remaining years in Egypt peacefully. When the

---

91. Cf. S.R. Hirsch, *op. cit.,* Bereshit 47:9.
92. Cf. Avraham ben Moshe, *Commentary on the Torah* (London 1958), Bereshit 47:9.

time came for him to depart from the world, he summoned together all his sons and blessed them. The Torah concludes the life of Yaakov with his last words:

> Then he instructed them, saying to them, "I am about to be gathered to my kin. Bury me with my fathers in the cave which is in the field of Efron the Hittite, the cave which is in the field of Machpelah, facing Mamre, in the land of Canaan, the field that Avraham bought from Efron the Hittite for a burial site. There Avraham and his wife Sarah were buried; there Yizhak and his wife Rivkah were buried; and there I buried Leah — the field, and the cave in it, bought from the Hittites." When Yaakov finished his instructions to his sons, he drew his feet into the bed and, breathing his last, he was gathered to his people.
>
> (Bereshit 49:29-33)

Part II

Moshe: The Man And His Mission

Introduction

Moshe Rabbenu . . . teacher, lawgiver, chief of prophets, spokesman of the Lord, defender of the Jewish people — the literature abounds in praise and in commentary on the noble pursuits of this charismatic leader. Where shall we begin his life story? What initial act made his life significant for the Jewish people? Was it when he showed his allegiance to Israel by killing the Egyptian who was beating an Israelite? Perhaps it was when he was saved by the hand of God from the Pharaoh's edict: "Every boy that is born you shall throw into the river, but let every girl live" (Shemot 1:22). It is difficult to determine where or when the life of Moshe becomes Jewish history. We shall begin at the end.

> So Moshe the servant of the Lord died there, in the land of Moav, at the command of the Lord. . . . And the Israelites bewailed Moshe in the steppes of Moav for thirty days . . .
>
> (Devarim 34:5, 8)

Wailing is the initial response to the irrevocable tragedy of death. It is the cry of pain. It is the emotional reaction to a loss most personal, which at the time is both unbelievable and unacceptable . . . a bad dream. For all intents and purposes, the reaction is uncontrollable and immune to the comforting words and gestures of well meaning friends. It is best left alone, to subside gradually with the passing of time. For time does, indeed, heal all wounds. Only the scar remains, causing minor twinges of pain from time to time, when lingering memories bring to mind the void . . . the irreparable loss.

Moshe was unique. The level of self-perfection he attained that prepared him for his Divine mission exceeded by far that which had been attained by any man before him, or has been attained by any man since. It was a state so sublime that it necessitated his being separated from both his own family and the masses of Israel. Indeed, he was a paradigm for the people of Israel among the nations, the people about whom Bilaam said, ". . . there is a people who dwells apart, not reckoned among the nations" (Bemidbar 23:9). Moshe dwelt alone . . . separate . . . specially consecrated by the Almighty. Yet, despite his uniqueness, or perhaps because of it, the Torah records: "And Moshe the man was more humble than any human being on the face of the earth" (Bemidbar 12:3).

The initial shock to the nation of Israel upon the death of Moshe abated, and the weeping and wailing ended. But the profundity of the loss — the effect it had on the condition and future direction of Israel — mounted greater and greater in the eyes of the people through the passing years, and the void remains. In secret, ever so quietly, the mourning continues.

In our studies, we will analyze the life of Moshe from the Biblical text as well as the writings of our Sages from early to modern times. We will concentrate on the three realms in which he excelled: his humanity, his leadership skills, and his prophetic ability. Although, for the most part, the incidents to which we will refer are spelled out, we advise the reader to familiarize himself with the Biblical texts.

Chapter 1

Beginnings

It is virtually impossible for one person to know another so well that he can evaluate the other's life with total objectivity — without being influenced to any extent by personal prejudices, either for or against him. To be sure, it is a noble goal towards which to strive, but to believe that one has achieved it is to indulge in self-delusion. Only the Almighty is truly objective. Couple this thought with the contention that the most valid criticism and judgment one obtains comes from his teacher or mentor, who knows him best, and it will become apparent that we are most fortunate in our studies here. We are privy to information on Moshe's life and an evaluation of his character written by his teacher and mentor — none other than the Almighty Himself. One illustration will suffice for the time being.

When Aharon and Miriam spoke slanderously against Moshe, the Lord summoned them to the Tent of Meeting and said: ". . . If there be a prophet among you, I the Lord make Myself known to him in a vision, I speak with him in a dream. Not so with My servant Moshe; he is trusted throughout My household. With him I speak mouth to mouth, plainly and not in riddles, and he beholds the likeness of the Lord . . ." (Bemidbar 12:6-8).

This was *Moshe Rabbenu,* the eighty-year-old sage and prophet who stood unafraid and determined before the awesome Pharaoh and demanded the release of the Israelites. But what were the beginnings of this charismatic figure? What were his inherent qualities, and what role was played by his environment in transforming Moshe the *child* into Moshe the *man* and finally Moshe the *Man of God?*

The stamina and determination that so characterize the personality of Moshe were preceded by his parents Amram and Yocheved who, despite the Pharaoh's edict that all male children to be born to the Israelites were to be killed, were determined to bring another child into the world.[1] It is not at all unlikely that their courage was conveyed to him by his sister Miriam when he reached the age of understanding, and that it affected and molded his approach to life.

It seems that, just as it was the destiny of the child Moshe to live, so was it his destiny to be raised away from his parents and his home. Indeed, he had to grow up away from the corruptive slave mentality of his brethren, who might have implanted within his personality the seeds of defeat — the posture of acquiescence to the lot of the downtrodden. So we read: "And the child grew and she brought him to the daughter of the Pharaoh, and he was adopted as a son. And she called him *Moshe,* for she drew him out of the water" (Shemot 2:10).

How mysterious are the ways of God! Moshe, the designated teacher of Israel, was to spend his formative years in the palace of the Pharaoh, the cruel monarch of Egypt, from whom he would be forced to flee as a young adult and before whom he would, in his old age, stand as an adversary. How strange that Moshe would be exposed to and master a culture that was in essence diametrically opposed to the principles of the Torah. Why? Was it to give him the ability to compare and contrast? To see the light from the darkness? The 12th century

---

1. Cf. Rashi, Shemot 2:1.

commentator Avraham Ibn Ezra opines that it was to implant within his heart a nobility of spirit and a respect for learning, but also that he needed to win the fear and allegiance of his brethren, who would not have accorded such to one of their own.[2] Indeed, a slave mentality does not lend itself to leadership. It should be noted here that, although Moshe acquired all the wisdom of Egypt and became a man of true royalty, he forgot neither his people nor his birthplace.[3]

The Torah speaks of Moshe as an infant, then as an adult who ventures out among his people to see their affliction. We are told nothing of his early years in the palace. For that information, we must turn to two post-Biblical sources: *Antiquities of the Jews*[4] and *Chronicles of Moshe Our Teacher.*[5]

The former is the work of Flavius Josephus, the first century Jewish historian. Josephus writes that Moshe was adopted by Thermuthis (Bitya), the daughter of the Pharaoh, after he was weaned by his mother Yocheved. Thermuthis loved him like a son and, seeing his brilliance, proposed that he be heir to the throne.[6] Josephus then records a powerful story regarding the Pharaoh's crown.[7] Seeing the

---

2. Cf. Avraham Ibn Ezra, Shemot 2:3.
3. Cf. M. Malbim, *Ha-Torah V'ha-Mizvah,* Shemot 2:10.
4. Flavius Josephus, *Antiquities of the Jews* (Philadelphia, 1957).
5. "Divre ha-Yamim L'Moshe Rabbenu," *Ozar Midrashim,* ed. J.D. Eisenstein (New York, 1956), Vol. I.
6. Josephus, *op. cit.,* Book II, Chapter X, p. 77.
7. *Ibid.* "Thermuthis, therefore perceiving him to be so remarkable a child, adopted him for her son, having no child of her own. And when one time she carried Moshe to her father, she showed him to him and said she thought to make him her father's successor, if it should please God she should have no legitimate child of her own; and said to him, 'I have brought up a child who is of a divine form and of a generous mind; and as I have received him from the bounty of the river, in a wonderful manner, I thought proper to adopt him for my son and the heir of thy kingdom.' And when she had said this, she put the infant into her father's

incident as an omen, the scribes advised the Pharaoh to have Moshe executed, but Thermuthis saved him.

Years passed. Ethiopia was at war with Egypt, winning battle after battle. With Egypt facing defeat, the oracles advised the Pharaoh that Moshe be made general of the army. Moshe was victorious in battle, winning the royal city of Saba, the last stronghold of Ethiopia, by promising to wed Tharbis, the king's daughter. After their marriage, Moshe returned to Egypt a hero, only to have his life again threatened, for killing an Egyptian — where the Torah picks up the story. Moshe was forced to flee to Midian.[8]

Another version of Moshe's involvement in Ethiopia is found in *Chronicles of Moshe Our Teacher.*[9] There, Moshe had already fled Egypt, and he fought on the side of the Ethiopians. Victorious in battle, the people elected Moshe as king (for the former king had died) and gave him the existing queen for a wife. But Moshe, loyal to the covenant with God, refused to live with her. Angry and frustrated, the queen persuaded the people to elect another king over them. Moshe was given wealth and valuables and he went to Midian.

---

hands. So he took him, and hugged him close to his breast, and on his daughter's account, in a pleasant way, put his crown upon his head. But Moshe threw it down to the ground and, in a puerile mood, he wreathed it round and trod upon it with his feet, which seemed to bring along with it an evil presage concerning the kingdom of Egypt."

8. *Ibid.,* pp. 77-78.
9. *Chronicles, op. cit.,* p. 375. This version is recorded by Y. Abravanel and Y.Z. Mecklenberg, who mention the source and consider it authoritative. One should be aware, however, of the comment made by Avraham Ibn Ezra on this work: "And that which is written in the *Chronicles of Moshe* is not to be believed. Let me give you a principle: Any book not written by the prophets or the Sages, from tradition, is not to be relied upon, particularly when it contains matters that contradict the proper meaning" (Shemot 2:22).

It is self-evident that the wisdom of Egypt — its arts and crafts and its knowledge of architecture — which Moshe had mastered, served as an enriching background from which he could more intelligently appreciate the construction of the Tabernacle in the wilderness. Yet, more importantly, His knowledge of Egyptian culture must have reinforced his appreciation of Torah law. As we have already pointed out, he must have compared and contrasted the two in his mind. How primitive was the culture of Egypt, zoomorphic in its conception of God — deifying bulls, crocodiles, and apes. How pale it must have been, indeed, when compared to the Torah principle of ethical monotheism. In Egypt, man was second to the beast and as such always in bondage. Human life had little value, and men were sacrificed to the idolatry of architectural achievement. How great a contrast when compared to the principles of human dignity found in the Torah, as manifest in the laws between man and his fellow man.

Greater and by far more important than Moshe's intellectual sophistication and charisma was his righteousness — his noble virtues — for it prepared him so well for the role he was to assume as leader of the nation of Israel. The Torah mentions these noble virtues at the start. We read: "And it came to pass in those days that Moshe grew up and went out to see his people; and he recognized their affliction" (Shemot 2:11). Moshe witnessed three incidents and reacted to each. He saw an Egyptian beating a Hebrew.[10] He saw two Hebrews fighting.[11] He saw seven shepherdesses who had come to draw water being driven away by the shepherds.[12] In each case, Moshe championed the cause of justice, pleading for the oppressed. An interesting analysis is given by

---

10. Cf. Shemot 2:11.
11. Cf. Shemot 2:13.
12. Cf. Shemot 2:16, 17.

Nehama Leibowitz, one of our contemporary master teachers of Torah.

Had the Torah only revealed the first incident, she says, one could argue that it was not Moshe's concern for justice that motivated his action, but rather his feelings for his brethren and his hatred for those who afflicted them. Had the second incident also been revealed, one could still argue that it was national pride that motivated him. It is the third incident — both the oppressed and the oppressors are strangers, and Moshe comes to the aid of the oppressed — which convinces us that Moshe's disdain for foul play motivated him to act.

His life threatened, Moshe escapes from Egypt and goes to Midian, where he becomes a shepherd, as were his forefathers. What is the significance of the apparent preoccupation of the patriarchs, as well as the prophets, of Israel with sheepherding? Is it merely coincidental? An insightful point is made by the 19th century commentator par excellence Shimshon Raphael Hirsch, in Bereshit 4:2. He writes:

> Pastoral life has its advantages; the fact that it deals only with living creatures, whose care and attention call for and keep alive all humane feelings of tenderness and consideration, is no small advantage. . . . The occupation does not make such a demand on the expenditure of actual strength, is not such a strain on the mind in service of the work, and gives the mind opportunity for elevating thoughts of Godliness and goodness. Thus we find our patriarchs as shepherds, and a Moshe and a David with the flocks.

The Midrash takes the nobility of sheepherding even further. It was the medium through which Moshe attained and demonstrated his true compassion, a trait indispensable for a leader. Thus we read:

> God does not grant greatness to a man until He tests him on a trivial

matter. . . . The Holy One Blessed Be He tested Moshe through his flocks. Our Sages tell us that when Moshe tended the flocks of Yitro in the wilderness a little calf began to stray, and Moshe chased after it. When it came to a brook, it stopped to drink. Observing it drinking, Moshe said, "I did not know that you strayed out of thirst. Surely you are now very tired." He put the calf on his shoulders and walked with it. Seeing him, the Holy One Blessed Be He said, "Your compassion compels you to treat your sheep in such a fashion. I promise you that in the future you will lead My sheep as well."

(Shemot Rabbah 2:2, 3)

These were some of the qualities of Moshe the man — courage, compassion, wisdom, and righteousness. They rendered him eminently qualified to assume the leadership role for which he was destined. But there was yet another quality of his that manifests itself from time to time in the Biblical narrative; it is an attribute found in the patriarch Avraham and the prophets of Israel, as well as in all the pious ones of Jewish history. It is first revealed to us in the Torah at the "burning bush." It is the attribute of humility.

Chapter 2

The Sacred Mission

Moshe was in the wilderness, tending the flock of his father-in-law Yitro, when he came upon a place the Torah calls Horev — the mountain of God. In the distance, he saw a blazing fire in a bush that somehow was not being consumed. Puzzled by this strange phenomenon, Moshe went to investigate the matter. As he approached the bush, the Almighty called out to him:

> "Moshe, Moshe!" He answered, "Here I am." And He said, "Do not come closer . . . I have marked well the plight of My people in Egypt . . . Come, therefore, I will send you to Pharaoh, and you shall free My people, the Israelites, from Egypt." But Moshe said to God, "Who am I that I should go to Pharaoh and free the Israelites from Egypt? . . . Please, Lord, I have never been a man of words, neither in times past nor now that You have spoken to Your servant: I am slow of speech and slow of tongue."
>
> (Shemot 3:4, 5, 7, 10, 11; 4:10)

Moshe entered the second stage of his life: his transformation from Moshe the man to Moshe the *Man of God.* How interesting! It is not man who finds God but God who finds man. And how remarkable it is that the sublime encounter with the Divine takes place not in some awesome palace or temple, but in the open wilderness — virgin

96

territory that does not yet bear the stamp of man's ruthless machinations. Let us also not forget that Moshe was tending the sheep at the time, an occupation we have already learned is most conducive to prophecy.

Our Sages tell us that in this initial encounter the Divine manifested Itself to Moshe through an angel. But what is an angel? The Hebrew term *mal'akh* means "messenger," according to Maimonides. Everyone who is entrusted with a mission is, in a sense, a *mal'akh.*[13] Some prophets saw angels in the form of man; others saw them as fire.[14]. In our context, the angel was the fire in the bush. Thus, it was not an ordinary fire, which explains why the bush was not consumed.

The incident raises an interesting question. God communicates with Moshe here through an intermediary . . . an angel. But have we not read that God communicated with Moshe directly? Indeed, God Himself said, concerning Moshe, "With him I speak mouth to mouth" (Bemidbar 12:8). Maimonides writes that this unique form of prophecy was what differentiated Moshe from the other prophets. While all other prophets perceived God in a dream or a vision, Moshe prophesied while awake. In Maimonides' words, "All other prophets perceived God through an angel; not so Moshe."[15]

The problem can be resolved through the approach of Rabbenu B'haye, the 13th century Spanish commentator par excellence. Since this was Moshe's first encounter with prophecy, Rabbenu B'haye explains, God wanted to initiate him gradually, raising him from one level to another until his mind was sufficiently trained to enable him to

---

13. Cf. Bereshit 32:4.
14. Cf. M. Maimonides, *Guide of the Perplexed,* Vol. II, pp. 38-40.
15. M. Maimonides, *Mishneh Torah:* Laws Concerning Foundations of the Torah 7:6.

tolerate a direct encounter. For this reason, this encounter was through the agency of an angel.[16]

The Lord calls out to Moshe. Upon hearing his name, Moshe hides his face in fright. Why? What was his fear? What could he possibly have seen? We will refer once again to the commentary of Meir L. Malbim, who in his unparalleled skill at textual analysis clarifies the meaning here. One must differentiate between the term *re'iyah*, which means "visual perception," and *habatah*, which means "intellectual perception." The latter term almost never pertains to sight. In our text, the term *habatah* is used, indicating intellectual perception. Moshe hid his face as a gesture of unpreparedness to perceive the words of God. Correctly, the verse should be read, ". . . and Moshe hid his face, for he was afraid *to perceive* God" (Shemot 3:6).[17]

At the burning bush, the Holy One Blessed Be He reveals to Moshe His plan to redeem the people of Israel, and the role Moshe will play in this plan. What is Moshe's reaction? Elation? Pride? Not at all. We read, "But Moshe said to God, 'Who am I that I should go to Pharaoh and free the Israelites from Egypt?' " (Shemot 3:11). Did this betray a lack of faith and trust in God? Highly unlikely. More reasonable would be the assumption that it was Moshe's humble assessment of his qualifications and an underestimation of his abilities. In a word, humility. Quite out of character for what one might have expected of so noble, so charismatic, so inspiring a figure as Moshe. Yet this was very much in character with the patriarchs of old and the prophets of Israel who were to follow. The pious never see themselves as such; perhaps therein lies their piety. How reminiscent of Avraham. Emerging victorious from the battle with the five kings, Avraham was terribly

---

16. Rabbenu B'haye, Shemot 3:1.
17. Cf. Malbim, *op. cit.,* Shemot 3:6.

depressed. Having been granted this victory, had all his righteousness been requited? Would this mean that he would no longer merit a son?[18] And did not the prophets of Israel also question their qualifications to be God's messengers? Such is the nature of Jewish righteousness.

The matter of questioning God, even for Moshe, is still problematic. When Moshe appears before Pharaoh, demanding the release of the Israelites, Pharaoh is enraged. He doubles the work of the Hebrew slaves, thereby worsening their condition. Incapable of fathoming God's ways, Moshe returns to God, complaining: ". . . why did You bring harm upon this people? Why did You select me? Ever since I came to Pharaoh to speak in Your name, it has gone worse with this people; yet, You have not delivered Your people at all" (Shemot 5:22, 23). How interestingly the Midrash depicts God's reaction to Moshe's words. It is with a feeling of disappointment rather than anger that God confronts His servant:

> The Holy One Blessed Be He said to Moshe: "Alas for those who are gone and no more to be found. How many a time I have revealed Myself to Avraham, Yizhak, and Yaakov with the name Almighty God, and I did not reveal to them My name 'Lord,' as I did to you; yet they did not inquire after My attributes. . . . As for you, at the onset of your mission you already inquired, 'What is Your name?' And now you say, 'Ever since I came to Pharaoh to speak in Your name, it has gone worse with this people.' "
>
> (Midrash Tanhuma: VaEra 1)

Here again, we must be apologetic. Moshe's fear and apprehension, his lack of confidence, and, finally, his confusion with the ways of God could only have been due to his lack of experience and his sensitivity to

---

18. Cf. Rashi, Bereshit 15:1.

the affliction of his people. The more Moshe threatened Pharaoh and saw these threats actualized by the Lord, the greater were his faith and convictions.

It was a new Moshe, unflinching in his determination and filled with self-confidence, who, when confronted with Pharaoh's question: "Who are the ones who will go to worship in the wilderness?" responded forthrightly, "With our young and with our old we shall go, with our sons and with our daughters, with our sheep and with our cattle we shall go, for we must observe the Lord's pilgrimage" (Shemot 10:8, 9). And once again, after the plague of darkness, in sheer audacity, "You yourself must provide us with sacrifices and burnt offerings to offer up to the Lord our God. Our own livestock, too, shall go along with us — not a hoof shall remain behind . . ." (Shemot 10:25, 26).

Moshe was, indeed, a man of power, courage, and determination, but he would not allow these qualities to swell his ego. Neither would he direct his efforts toward personal concerns or self-aggrandizement. He remained Moshe the Pious, most concerned with the fulfillment of God's word and the promises made to his forefathers, which became his destiny to fulfill.

When the time came to leave Egypt, Moshe sought out the remains of Yosef and took them with him for burial in Canaan, for Yosef had foresworn the people of Israel to do this thing. While all Israel concerned themselves with silver and gold, tells us the Midrash, Moshe concerned himself with the remains of Yosef.

> Said the Holy One Blessed Be He, "Yosef was obligated to bury his father, for he was a son. But you are neither a son nor a grandson (of Yosef) and you were not obligated to concern yourself with him, yet you buried him; I, too, am not obligated to any creature, but I will busy Myself with you (your burial)."
>
> (Shemot Rabbah 20:17)

Moshe's experience in Egypt, his maiden voyage on the sea of prophecy, enriched his comprehension of providence. What had once perplexed him to the point where he had audaciously questioned the ways of God was adequately resolved. Therefore, at the Red Sea, he had only words of praise to offer to the Almighty: "I will sing to the Lord for He has triumphed gloriously; horse and rider He has hurled into the sea" (Shemot 15:1).

Onward, to the land of Canaan!

Chapter 3

The Sin of the Golden Calf

Israel embarked on what was to become a forty-year journey through the wilderness to the land of Canaan, and Moshe took on a new role. From Moshe the man had come Moshe the Man of God; now, from Moshe the Man of God came Moshe *leader par excellence*. He was no ordinary leader, no commonplace general who would use his position for personal gain or advantage. He always put the welfare of the people of Israel above personal comforts and considerations, and their protection above even his own survival. Right or wrong, they were the people of Israel, the Lord's treasure. They had to survive. Yes, they were sinners at times, but they had to be forgiven.

Witness Moshe's words to God after the horrendous sin of the golden calf: "Alas, this people is guilty of a great sin in making for themselves a god of gold. And yet, if You would only forgive their sin! If not, erase me from the book which You have written" (Shemot 32:31, 32). Could one have expected more then, or as much today? Whence did such feelings of devotion and compassion derive? The Midrash relates these qualities to Moshe's occupation, and the analogy rings a familiar note:

To whom can Moshe our teacher be likened? To a faithful shepherd who returned his flock at dusk to their protective enclosure and noticed that it had fallen down. Quickly he repaired it on three sides. Time did not suffice to repair the fourth side, and it remained open. Anticipating imminent danger, he put himself in its place. A lion came and he stood up against it; a wolf came and he stood up against it.

(Rut Rabbah: Introduction)

Patience was one of Moshe's most noble virtues. How many leaders would have thrown up their hands in despair when faced with some of the faithless, rebellious acts of this stubborn and stiff-necked people. Not so Moshe; he persevered. He had to train Israel in the most basic rules of conduct and the most fundamental principles of worship. He remained with them, eager and undaunted. Two Midrashim will suffice to illustrate the condition of the Israelites at the time:

And Moshe said, "It is the Lord who will give you flesh to eat in the evening and bread in the morning to the full . . ." (Shemot 16:8). Said R. Acha: At first the children of Israel were like roosters who pick at the garbage. Then Moshe came and designated times for meals.

(Yoma 75b)

When Israel was ready to recite the song of praise to God at the Red Sea, Moshe did not allow them to recite it by themselves. Just as a child repeats after his teacher, they repeated after him . . .

(Yalkut Shimoni 5364)

As a leader par excellence, Moshe knew his people well. He knew when to plead their cause and when to admonish them, when to hold his ground with the Almighty and when to refuse to listen to the people's complaints. This point will enable us to understand the incident at Masah U'Merivah.

The Israelites journeyed from the wilderness of Sin and encamped at Rephidim. They complained to Moshe that there was no water, and he responded, "Why do you quarrel with me? Why do you test the Lord?" (Shemot 17:1, 2). How strange. Moshe curt and impatient? In truth, says Naftali Zvi Yehudah Berlin, the 19th century Polish talmudist and exegete, the problem was not with their thirsting; they had not thirsted, but only complained that there was no water to drink. Moshe understood that they were merely testing the Lord to see if He could supply them with water. They did not thirst for water. He therefore rebuked them and revealed their thinking. This silenced their murmuring.[19] The verses that follow are the proof: "And the people thirsted there for water and grumbled against Moshe . . . And Moshe cried out to the Lord: What shall I do with this people? A little more of this and they will stone me" (Shemot 17:3, 4). When they truly thirsted and their complaint was valid, Moshe immediately pleaded their cause.

It is important to understand the significance of Moshe's choice of words, viz., "A little more of this and they will stone me." A most enlightening comment is made by the renowned German sage of the 19th century Yaakov Zvi Mecklenberg. It was not Moshe's fear of being stoned to death that motivated him to cry out to the Lord, but rather his feeling that this time their complaint was legitimate. Moshe felt that if he waited much longer — to the point where their thirst became unbearable — they might do something quite dramatic. Were such the case, he would not have considered it an impropriety had they tried to humiliate him by pelting him with stones.[20]

Confirmation of our approach to this matter may be found in the strange juxtaposition of the battle of Amalek to this incident of the

---

19. Cf. N.Z.Y. Berlin, *Ha'amek Davar,* Shemot 17:1, 2.
20. Cf. Y.Z. Mecklenberg, *Ha-Ketav V'ha-Kabbalah,* Shemot 17:4.

murmuring.[21] Now, while the Midrash regards this as an indication that the confrontation was a punishment of the Israelites for their sin,[22] it may also have been meant to teach us a crucial fact about Moshe's leadership. Despite the murmuring of the people, which might have motivated another leader to anger and consequent withdrawal from concern for their welfare, Moshe remained their advocate and their confidant. This is illustrated in the battle of Amalek. As long as the people could see Moshe's hands raised high in prayer, they were inspired and successful in battle. Moshe knew that if he would lower his hands it could be disastrous for the people; he therefore had Aharon and Hur support his arms throughout the battle, rather than see bloodshed and chance defeat of the army of Israel. Indeed, there is a time for loving and a time for hating . . . a time for tearing down and a time for building up. To recognize this and to put it into proper practice is what makes for great leadership.

We have already noted that Moshe was a strong-willed and charismatic individual, who possessed both the wisdom and the talent necessary to influence and affect his fellow man. A case in point is his father-in-law Yitro. Yitro was a man of great substance and power in his own right; he was, in fact, the high priest of Midian. It would seem from the Torah text that he was a man of wisdom as well, as he advises Moshe to initiate a judicial system so that he might avoid the tediousness of having to handle every domestic and social problem himself. Bearing this in mind, we can safely assume that when a discussion ensued between the two men it was an exchange of sophisticated ideas. Convincing Yitro to renounce both his position and his idolatrous beliefs and commit himself to God and to Torah must

---

21. Cf. Shemot 17:8-13.
22. Cf. *Midrash Tanhuma,* Yitro 3.

have taken carefully calculated arguments and presumably much discussion. Who knows how many more people were brought by Moshe under the wings of the Divine Presence?

When Moshe sent for his family to join him in the wilderness, Yitro came with them. The two men greeted each other warmly. We then read:

> And Moshe told his father-in-law all that the Lord had done to Pharaoh and Egypt for Israel's sake, all the hardships that had befallen them. And Yitro rejoiced over all the good that the Lord had done to Israel in delivering them from the Egyptians. And Yitro said: "Blessed be the Lord who delivered you from the Egyptians and from Pharaoh and who delivered the people from under the hand of the Egyptians. Now I know that the Lord is greater than all gods . . ."
> (Shemot 18:8-12)

Yitro departs with Moshe's good wishes and with the words we find in the Midrash: "I am returning to my country to convert all its citizens, to bring them to a commitment to study the Torah, and to thereby earn the protection of the Divine Presence."[23]

Such was the power of Moshe, the dynamic and charismatic leader. On a "one to one" basis, he was superb.

But how did Moshe fare with the masses — the generation of former slaves who, by the nature of their condition, were prone to primitive thinking and suspicion? Let us recall what was perhaps the most horrendous event in the journey of the Israelites to Canaan — the incident of the golden calf.

The awesome and impressive revelation on Mount Sinai

---

23. Cf. *Mekhilta,* Shemot 18:27.

notwithstanding, when the people saw that Moshe tarried in descending the mountain, they panicked. They came to Aharon and demanded that he make them a tangible god to lead them. Hoping to dissuade them from this impropriety, or at least to delay them long enough for Moshe to return, he instructed them to bring him their gold rings and those of their families. But the ploy did not work. Under duress, Aharon fashioned the golden calf, and when the people saw it they shouted, "This is your god, O Israel!" The next day, they sacrificed, ate, and made merry in its honor.[24]

Uprooted from the polytheistic and zoomorphic culture in which they, their parents, and their grandparents had lived — a span of 210 years — and led into the wilderness by a man whom they, as yet, did not really know, they were confused. Much like the helpless child who, when faced with a situation he cannot handle, cries hysterically because he knows no other way to react, so too did the Israelites, when faced with the traumatic prospect of being left without a leader — which to them meant without a God — resort to the only thing they knew well: the culture of Egypt and the tangible god. It was a sad day in Jewish history.

How was Moshe made aware of what had happened, and how did he handle the situation?

Moshe was still on the mountain. The Lord spoke to him once more, not to reveal the Law, but to bring him the tragic news: "Hurry down, for your people, whom you brought out from the land of Egypt, have acted basely" (Shemot 32:7). The Talmud comments: "Hurry down, descend from your position of greatness. Have I at all given you

---

24. Cf. Shemot 18:27.

greatness but for the sake of Israel? And now Israel has sinned; then why do I want you?"[25]

How disparaging a remark to so devoted a leader! We will not be so presumptuous as to attempt to fathom God's motivation. But note the words "for your people." Indeed, the Torah speaks in the language of man. Like one parent to another, when the children are good, they are *our* children; when they are bad, they are *yours*.

But it is the "Lord," *Hashem,* who speaks to Moshe. The name "Lord" is traditionally associated with the attribute of mercy, and the fulfillment of the promises that were made to the patriarchs.[26] It is the symbolism implied in this name of God that gave Moshe the confidence he needed to plead for Israel. The Midrash focuses on God's subsequent words: "I have seen this people; they are a stubborn lot. Now let Me be, that My anger may blaze forth against them and that I may destroy them and make of you a great nation" (Shemot 32:10). The Midrash comments: "Moshe had not yet prayed for them and God says, 'Let Me be'? Here God gave Moshe the opening to intercede, and indicated that the matter was in his hands. If he prayed for them, they would not be destroyed."[27]

How does Moshe approach this herculean task?

Retreat in the face of assault is the forerunner of defeat. Moshe stands firm on behalf of his people and presents his defense. According to the Midrash, he reasoned thus: If I leave the matter of Israel status quo and descend from the mountain, they will surely be destroyed. I will not budge from here until I plead for mercy on their behalf.[28] Quite a

---

25. Berakhot 32a.
26. Cf. Rashi, Shemot 6:2.
27. Cf. Rashi, Shemot 32:10.
28. Cf. *Shemot Rabbah* 42:1.

change from the Moshe who had once pleaded: "They will not believe me; they will not hearken to my voice. Please, Lord, I have never been a man of words, neither in times past nor now that You have spoken to Your servant; I am slow of speech and slow of tongue" (Shemot 4:10).

The prestigious Don Yizhak Abravanel, the Biblical commentator of 15th century Spain, points out that when Moshe heard God's plan to utterly destroy the Jewish people he tried desperately to appease His anger. Those who have sinned should indeed be punished, he argued, but not the rest of the community with them.[29] How reminiscent of Avraham's defense of the city of Sodom.

And so, Moshe begins his skilled, multifaceted defense of the nation of Israel:

> "Let not Your anger, O Lord, blaze forth against Your people, whom You have delivered from the land of Egypt with great power and with a mighty hand."
>
> (Shemot 32:11)

The Midrash records much more of this opening conversation between God and Moshe:

> Said R. Shmuel: Moshe said to God: "Lord of the universe, give me permission to speak." Said the Holy One Blessed Be He: "Speak whatever you wish." Moshe then said: "The Israelites have indeed nullified the first part of the second commandment, 'You shall have no other gods beside Me,' by making the calf. Now You wish to nullify the latter half: 'I show kindness to the thousandth generation of those who love Me and keep My commandments'? Is it not

---

29. Cf. Y. Abravanel, Shemot 32, p. 315.

109

written, '(They are) the seed of Avraham, My beloved'? You said to Avraham, 'I will show kindness to your children for two thousand generations.' How many generations have passed from Avraham till now? Seven! Avraham, Yizhak, Yaakov, Levi, Kehat, Amram, Moshe."

(Shemot Rabbah 44:7)

The argument is quite logical. Destruction of the nation of Israel would be contrary to God's promise to Avraham. What appears illogical, however, is the statement "Your people, whom You have delivered from the land of Egypt with great power and with a mighty hand." Why the need to remind God of His deed? Surely this is superfluous, unless the emphasis here is not on the redemption, but on the enslavement. Perhaps Moshe meant to stress the great impact the Egyptian culture had on the Israelites. They had lived for 210 years in a culture steeped in idolatry. What could one have expected of them when the going got tough? Man is a victim of his environment and, at least to some extent, its product. This must certainly be taken into account in administering justice. Man is weak; he often fails to repel negative influences. True, justice demands punishment, in the strictest sense. But the Torah tells us that when man was created God began to relate to the world through His attribute of justice tempered with mercy. Man could not have survived otherwise.[30]

The defense continues:

"Why should the Egyptians say: 'It is with evil intent that He delivered them, to kill them off in the mountains and annihilate them from the face of the earth'?"

(Shemot 32:12)

---

30. Cf. *Shemot Rabbah* 43.8.

The point here is not that God should be concerned with what the Egyptians think or say. Of what import would that be to Him? It is rather that the destruction of Israel would mean the termination of her mission — which would have a devastating effect on humanity. Man was put on this earth to acknowledge and serve his Creator. He was endowed with freedom of will and charged to choose good over evil. Early man chose to deny God, however, and serve his own evil inclination instead. Only the family of Avraham recognized the one God and the principle of ethical monotheism, to which they dedicated their lives. Therefore, they were chosen to become God's nation and charged to set the example for all mankind, eventually initiating a return of all mankind to God. Hence, according to God's plan, it was important that Israel remain alive and viable.[31]

Lastly, should all of his arguments fail to win the pardon he desired, Moshe appealed to God in the merit of the patriarchs: Avraham, Yizhak, and Yaakov.

> "Remember Avraham, Yizhak, and Yaakov, to whom You promised in Your name, saying: 'I will multiply your seed like the stars in the heavens.' "
>
> (Shemot 32:13)

What is the significance of the appeal to *zechut avot,* "the merit of the forefathers"?

The patriarchs have a strange and unique power over the destiny of the nation of Israel. It is as though they have ingratiated themselves in God's heart to such an extent that mere mention of their names is

---

31. Cf. Ramban, Devarim 32:26.

sufficient to achieve the desired goal. Eliyahu the prophet offered many prayers on Mount Carmel without being answered, but when he addressed the Almighty as the God of Avraham, Yizhak, and Yaakov, he was answered immediately. Moshe tried in all ways to exonerate Israel and failed; when he mentioned the patriarchs, he was answered immediately.[32] The Midrash explains this phenomenon as unrequited merit that works in behalf of Israel.

> Said Moshe: "Master of the universe! Why are You angry with Israel?" He said: "Because they have transgressed the Ten Commandments." Moshe said: "But they have from whom to demand repayment." He said: "From whom?" Moshe said: "Remember that You proved Avraham with ten trials (and he was not fully rewarded). Let those ten pay for these ten."[33]
>
> (Shemot Rabbah 44:4)

God's response? "And the Lord renounced the punishment He had planned to bring upon His people" (Shemot 32:14).

Let us backtrack a bit in our analysis of this event.

Moshe descends the mount bearing the Tablets in hand and witnesses the horrendous scene below. In what appears to be a thoughtless moment, he dashes the Tablets to the ground and smashes them to bits. Quite atypical of the Moshe that has been thus far revealed to us in the Torah: the devoted shepherd of the flock of Israel. Let us offer two interesting approaches:

Nahmanides explains quite simply that Moshe could not restrain himself. Coming down from the mountain, witnessing the shocking

---

32. Cf. *Shemot Rabbah* 44:1.
33. Cf. Rashi, Shemot 32:13.

event, his anger surfaced and he smashed the Tablets. Indeed, his refined human sensitivities could not tolerate this blatant desecration of God's name. The great leader who had until now borne the complaints of Israel with superhuman patience "lost his cool." He who had confronted God with the words "Let not Your anger burst forth . . . turn from Your blazing anger" now allowed himself that very expediency.[34]

The approach of Naftali Zvi Yehudah Berlin is entirely different. Moshe was truly enraged, says R. Berlin, but he did not lose his control. Quite the contrary. The text comes to explain how Moshe was able to take the calf and burn it, and not a single voice was raised in protest. God informed Moshe about the golden calf while the latter was still on the mountain. He wisely maintained control and withheld himself from smashing the Tablets right on the spot. The rationale was quite simple, says R. Berlin. He wanted to dramatize the act — to break the hearts of the people and terrify them as they witnessed the smashing of the Tablets, this priceless treasure. They would be so shocked with what they saw and so thoroughly appalled at themselves that they would not protest against anything Moshe did thereafter.[35]

Indeed, it was a grievous sin that the Israelites had committed, an act by which they forfeited their right to God's Law, and it is thus of the utmost importance that we clarify just exactly what that sin was.

Whether it was another leader that they wanted, as some suggest, or a tangible god, as others contend, the Israelites demanded a hand in their destiny. They refused to accept a God who would not meet *their* qualifications of time and space. So they constructed one to meet those

---

34. Cf. Ramban 32:16.
35. Cf. N.Z.Y. Berlin, *op. cit.,* Shemot 32:15.

demands. Needless to say, such a philosophy is diametrically opposed to Jewish thinking. This, too, was expressed by Moshe when he smashed the Tablets. It is either Torah or idolatry. If the choice is idolatry, there is no room, nor is there need, for the Torah.

But there was still another facet of the sin that motivated Moshe's behavior. As long as pagan ideas were restricted to incorrect thinking, there was still hope that reeducation could bring truth to light. When thought gave birth to action, however, expressing itself in behavior that was blatantly immoral, hope waned for effecting a meaningful change. This point is made quite eloquently by Shimson Raphael Hirsch in Shemot 32:19. He writes:

> As long as Moshe knew of the calf and its worship, he hoped that he would still be able to make a pure home amongst the people for the Torah, and he took the testimony of the Torah down with him. But when he saw the calf and the dances around it, then he realized how the pagan erroneous theories had borne their usual fruit, the shaking off of the restraining yoke of morality, unchaining sensuality. Then he saw that a nation would first have to be entirely reestablished for this Torah, and without any hesitation he cast the Tablets into pieces . . .

As dramatic and impressive as was the smashing of the Tablets, so was the destruction of the golden calf. It was a sensuous experience as regards the participation of the nation, but its message was clearly directed to the intellect. Abravanel expains that whatever Moshe did with the calf was done to make it an object of humiliation in the eyes of the people. Where Aharon had taken their little rings and fashioned them into a massive form — the calf — Moshe destroyed it and ground it into small particles of dust. Where they exclaimed, "This is your god, O Israel," Moshe initiated its destruction before their very eyes —

scattering the ashes on the waters and commanding them to drink of those waters so that they would void this abominable object from their bodies.[36]

There is another approach to the symbolism. According to tradition, the nation of Israel is symbolically wedded to God; serving another god is a manifestation of unfaithfulness of profound proportions. The national sin of idolatry is thus likened to adultery.[37] Here, Israel was being put through the test of the *sotah,* the unfaithful wife, to establish that point in the minds of the people.[38]

Now, what was the significance of the mass execution that took place afterwards? Three thousand people were killed. By whose authority was this done? According to the Torah text, Moshe tells the Israelites the following: "Thus says the Lord, God of Israel: 'Each of you put sword on thigh. Go back and forth from gate to gate throughout the camp and slay brother, neighbor, and kin' " (Shemot 32:27).

These words are somewhat puzzling. Just where and when did God give such a command to Moshe? Rashi asks the question and answers: "In the verse 'Whosoever sacrifices to a god other than the Lord shall be proscribed' " (Shemot 22:19). Further in the Torah, this punishment is interpreted as the death penalty.[39] It was not that God commanded Moshe on the scene. Rather, Moshe was simply carrying out one of the 613 commandments. We must note that Nahmanides disagrees with Rashi here, claiming that the Israelites could not be held guilty since

---

36. Cf. Y. Abravanel, Shemot 32, p. 318.
37. Cf. M. Malbim, *op. cit.,* Shemot 32:20, also Ramban *ad loc.*
38. Cf. Shemot 32:20 and Bemidbar 5:11-28.
39. "No human being who has been proscribed can be ransomed: he shall be put to death" (VaYikra 27:29).

they had not been forewarned. Moshe's action was *hora'at sha'ah,* an emergency measure taken because of the importance of sanctifying God's name.[40]

All the preliminary steps having been taken, Moshe turns to Israel with the words: "You have been guilty of a great sin. Yet, I will now go up to the Lord; perhaps I may win forgiveness for your sin" (Shemot 32:30).

Still an unrequited sin? Hadn't they been punished enough? Apparently not. True, many individuals of the nation had been severely penalized, but the nation as a whole had not yet been properly chastised for the sin of impropriety.

This was because Moshe was not chastising them at this point for their rebellious act of idolatry. Three thousand of the guilty ones had already been executed, many others had been proved guilty through the waters, and the rest would be executed by the Almighty Himself through a plague that would be inflicted upon them. It was rather for their impropriety — the magical thinking and fallacious reasoning that they needed a tangible god to lead them — that they were being chastised. It was for this sin that they now needed atonement.[41]

Moshe returns to the Lord to seek forgiveness for his people and the Torah records his startling words: "Alas, this people is guilty of a great sin in making for themselves a god of gold. And yet, if You would only forgive their sin! If not, erase me from the book which You have written" (Shemot 32:31, 32).

An ultimatum from Moshe? This seems very much out of character. Perhaps he felt that he had finally reached the point of no return. He was not at all interested in becoming the leader of a *new* nation, as God

---

40. Cf. Ramban, Shemot 32:27.
41. Cf. N.Z.Y. Berlin, *op. cit.,* Shemot 32:30.

had suggested. If it could not be Israel, it *would not* be Moshe. Perhaps he had lost confidence in his leadership ability. According to Yaakov Zvi Mecklenberg, what Moshe meant was that if it were not within God's will to forgive their sin the name "Moshe" should be erased from God's record of history, so that it would never be known among the nations of the world that Moshe, the shepherd leader of the people of Israel, had failed in his mission.[42]

Ultimatum or not, Moshe accomplished his goal, for the Lord responds: "He who has sinned against Me, him only will I erase from My book. But go now, lead the people where I told you. Moreover, My angel shall lead you" (Shemot 32:33, 34).

This was leadership par excellence! To put one's life on the line before the Almighty on behalf of a people who were stubbornly and consistently disobedient — a nation with whom even God seemed to have lost patience — took not only great courage and abounding love, but a discerning eye for the future as well.

The remaining sinners were executed through the plague, and the Israelites made ready to move on. Yet, all was not well. A vital change had been initiated by God which neither Moshe nor the people were prepared to accept. We read:

> Then the Lord said to Moshe, "Go, depart hence, you and the people you have brought from the land of Egypt, to the land of which I swore to Avraham, Yizhak, and Yaakov, saying, 'To your offspring will I give it.' I will send an angel before you . . . but I will not go in your midst, since you are a stiff-necked people, lest I destroy you on the way." When the people heard this harsh word, they went into mourning and none put on his finery.
>
> (Shemot 33:1-4)

---

42. Cf. Y.Z. Mecklenberg, *op. cit.*, 32:32.

Yes, the journey to the Promised Land of Canaan would continue, but the presence of the Lord would be manifested differently. The nation of Israel would hereafter be led by an angel. Whatever the significance of this change may have been, it apparently affected the people quite seriously, for it plunged them into mourning.

Why was the change necessary? It would seem that the horrendous sin had to take some toll on the relationship between the Almighty and His people, despite the relentless pleading of Moshe. R. Mecklenberg explains that, in truth, it was a manifestation of mercy on God's part. Had God accompanied the nation directly, they would have stood the chance of being annihilated. Their continuous stubbornness would have incurred God's wrath. Punishment of this sort, however, could not have been executed by an angel.[43]

How ironic. An event that was initiated through God's ultimate closeness to the people of Israel ended with the withdrawal of His personal providence. The election of the nation of Israel as the "chosen people," its redemption from Egypt, and the revelation to it of the Torah — all of which were manifestations of the most special Divine providence, promising the most wondrous future for this nation — seemed to have been forgotten in the blunder of a moment's weakness.

Even Moshe now felt that the Divine Presence would not rest upon him when he was within the camp of Israel, so he removed his tent from their midst and pitched it outside, at a distance — ". . .whoever sought the Lord would go out to the Tent of Meeting that was outside the camp" (Shemot 33:7). Rashi comments most poignantly: "One who has been banished by the teacher is simultaneously banished by the disciple."

---

43. *Ibid.,* Shemot 33:4.

The withdrawal of Moshe from the camp was short-lived, however. God was displeased with the decision, which Moshe had made of his own volition. The Midrash reveals some harsh words from the Almighty to His beloved disciple:

> The Holy One said to Moshe: "Did I not tell you that when I am angry with them you must show favor and when you are angry with them I will show favor? Now both you and I are angry with them. . . . Return to them and return to the camp. Do not come out of the camp to call to Me and then return . . ."
>
> (Midrash Tanhuma: Ki Tisa 27)

Relentless, Moshe is still disturbed by God's decision to send an angel to accompany the people of Israel to the land of Canaan. Perhaps the fault was his own, his inability to comprehend God's ways. Once more Moshe confronts the Lord:

> See, You say to me, "Lead this people forward," but You have not made known to me whom You will send with me. Further, You have said, "I have singled you out by name, and you have, indeed, gained My favor." Now if I have truly gained Your favor, pray let me know Your ways, that I may know You and continue in Your favor. Consider, too, that this nation is Your people.
>
> (Shemot 33:12, 13)

The meaning of these verses and their interrelationship is somewhat puzzling, and we must turn to the 16th century Polish exegete R. Eliezer Ashkenazi for an explanation of Moshe's words. He says:

> You tell me that You will send an angel with me. But when You made me Your messenger, You did not tell me that You want to send

someone with me, but rather that You Yourself would come with
me. . . . And You also said that You made Yourself known to me
by name and that I found favor in Your eyes. . . . When Moshe
saw that his request: "If you would only forgive their sin! If not, erase
me from the book which You have written" went unheeded, he
realized that the fault was his own, that he did not know how to
appease the Lord, for he didn't comprehend His ways.

(Ma'ase Hashem: Ki Tisa 13)

The Lord softens the impact of His decree and informs Moshe that
the angel that would accompany them would blend justice with mercy
in determining their plight. Still not appeased, Moshe counters: "If
Your Presence does not lead us, do not make us leave this place"
(Shemot 33:15).

Stubborn? Audacious? Perhaps. But never on his own behalf. It is
always on behalf of the people of Israel, for whom he felt full
responsibility, that Moshe spoke aggressively. Again, Moshe prevailed.

"And God said to Moshe, 'I will also do this thing that you have
asked, for you have truly gained My favor and I have singled you out
by name.' "

(Shemot 33:17)

The request to know God's ways not yet having been addressed,
Moshe puts forth a second request: "Oh, let me perceive Your essence"
(Shemot 33:18). The first request had been to comprehend the ways in
which God's will is made manifest in the world; the second was to
know His essence. God responds to the first request with the words:

"I will make all My goodness pass before you: I will be gracious to
whom I will be gracious and show compassion to whom I will show
compassion."

(Shemot 33:19)

What is the meaning of this response? How did it answer Moshe's request for understanding? The revered 18th century Bible commentator Hayyim ben Atar explains the verse as follows:

> What is implied here are the Divine attributes through which God is benevolent to His creatures. The phrase "before you" here means "because of you." Because of your great love and desire for Me, I will cause My attributes to pass before you and I will call them out by name, one by one. . . .
>
> (Or ha-Hayyim 33:19)

God promises Moshe to reveal and demonstrate to him His Divine attributes. But even more, he will grant Moshe the ability to comprehend the Divine goodness by allowing the entire creation to pass before Moshe's eyes. Creation is the supreme manifestation of God's goodness. God will declaim His attributes to Moshe's ears and by doing so trigger a mechanism that will bring even greater goodness into the world.[44]

Disappointingly, yet quite realistically, Moshe's second request was denied. No human being, not even Moshe, could perceive God's essence. And so Moshe draws a negative response: "You may not see My face, for man may not see Me and live" (Shemot 33:20).

What was it that Moshe had requested from God? Maimonides enlightens us here:

> He sought to have so clear an apprehension of the truth of God's existence that the knowledge might be like that which one possesses of a human being, whose face one has seen and whose image is imprinted on the mind, and whom, therefore, the mind distinguishes

---

44. M. Malbim, *op. cit.,* Shemot 33:19.

from other men. In the same way, Moshe our teacher asked that the truth of God's existence might be distinguished in his mind from other beings, and that he might thus know the truth of God's existence as it really is.

(Mishneh Torah: Laws Concerning
Foundations of the Torah 1:10)

Moshe's request is not totally rejected, however, for the Lord makes the following compromise:

See, there is a place near Me. Station yourself on the rock and, as My essence passes by, I will put you in a cleft of the rock and shield you with My hand, until I have passed by. Then I will take My hand away, and you will see My back, but My face must not be seen.

(Shemot 33:21-23)

Here, too, Maimonides explains: to know the essence of God is beyond the intellectual capacity of man, who is composed of body and soul. Yet, God now imparted to Moshe more knowledge of the Divine than He had heretofore imparted to any human being. This is implied in the words "you will see My back." Maimonides writes: "Moshe attained so much knowledge of the truth of the Divine existence that God was, in his mind, distinct from other beings, in the same way as an individual, whose back is seen, whose physical form and apparel are perceived, is distinguished in the observer's mind from the physical form of other individuals."[45]

---

45. M. Maimonides, *Mishneh Torah:* Laws Concerning Foundations of the Torah 1:10. One must be careful not to attribute any physical characteristics to God's essence, particularly in the writings of Maimonides, who in this very work teaches that one who does so is considered a heretic. Cf. Laws Concerning Repentance 3:7.

An interesting interpretation of the symbolism of the "back" of the Divine is given by the venerable contemporary theologian Joseph B. Soloveitchik. God's ways are often incomprehensible in the present, says R. Soloveitchik, because we are too emotionally involved, too subjective to see things in their true perspective. Only with the passage of time — years, sometimes generations — when emotional biases have been neutralized, when we can transcend an event and look at it objectively — do God's ways become intelligible to us. As such, Moshe was taught that God's ways in the world do not always seem just when viewed from the limited perspective of the present, and in the heat of the moment. It is as if the hand of God covers us, obscuring our understanding. In retrospect, however, when God has passed by, His hand is removed from our eyes and hindsight interpretation makes His ways intelligible, indeed, credible. Yes, says the Almighty, "you will see My back, but My face will not be seen."[46]

---

46. This material is taken from a lecture delivered at Yeshiva University on Purim 1974.

Chapter 4

The Beams on Moshe's Face

The Lord commands Moshe to prepare a second set of Tablets and to ascend the mountain once more. This time, he ascends the mountain without any fanfare. There is no thunder and lightning. Once again, the Ten Commandments are inscribed upon the Tablets, and Moshe takes leave of the Lord's Presence. Bearing the Tablets, he descends the mountain. The people see him from a distance and witness a strange phenomenon. The Torah records:

> And as Moshe came down from the mountain bearing the Two Tablets of the testimony, Moshe was not aware that the skin of his face was radiant because he had spoken with Him. Aharon and all the Israelites saw that the skin of Moshe's face was radiant, and they shrank from coming near him. But Moshe called to them, and Aharon and all the chieftains in the assembly returned to him, and Moshe spoke to them. Afterwards, all the Israelites came near, and he instructed them concerning all that the Lord had imparted to him on Mount Sinai. And when Moshe had finished speaking with them, he put a veil over his face.
>
> (Shemot 34:29-33)

How intriguing is this mysterious radiance of Moshe's face. How strange was its function. When Moshe spoke with the Lord, he would bare his face, and when he brought the Lord's message to the people, he would do so as well. At all other times, however, his face was veiled.

The Michelangelo *Moses,* by the 16th century artist of the Italian Renaissance, depicting the prophet with horns, stands out as perhaps the most horrendous misrepresentation of this event.[47] The phenomenon does not readily lend itself to investigation. As such, pictures or sculptures are not only of little value, but they are quite audacious. Let one remark suffice, therefore, concerning the Michelangelo error. Though it is true that the term *karnayim* in Hebrew usually means "horns," from the context it is apparent that what is meant here is "rays" or "beams."[48]

What is the symbolic significance of the beams on Moshe's face? Here there is some literature of interest. We shall examine it and offer an interpretation of our own.

The difference between the prophecy of Moshe and that of the other prophets of Israel is a qualitative one. Joseph B. Soloveitchik makes the point that since Maimonides, in his *Thirteen Principles of Faith*[49], lists the belief in the prophecy of Moshe as a separate principle, it is in a category of its own.[50] The Torah implies this as well. When, later in the Scriptural narrative, Miriam and Aharon speak against Moshe, they are suddenly confronted by the Lord, who rebukes them with the following words:

> Hear now My words: If there be a prophet among you, I the Lord make Myself known to him in a vision, I speak with him in a dream.

---

47. This blatant misrepresentation was probably due to the Vulgate translation of the Bible, which reads here, "His face sent out horns of light."
48. Cf. Habakkuk 3:3, 4.
49. M. Maimonides, *Commentary to the Mishnah,* Sanhedrin X, Principle 4.
50. Yevamot 49b. Cf. J.B. Soloveitchik, "Mah Dodekh Mi-Dod," *B'sod ha-Yahid V'ha-Yahad, op. cit.,* p. 205.

Not so with My servant Moshe; he is trusted throughout My household. With him I speak mouth to mouth, plainly and not in riddles, and he beholds the likeness of the Lord . . .

(Bemidbar 12:6-8)

The uniqueness of Moshe manifested itself in the character of that which was revealed to him by God. Moshe's perceived word became Torah; no prophet was permitted to add or delete from it. The uniqueness of the Torah is in its designation by God to be of ultimate validity to the Jewish people; hence its immutability. This immutability is what motivated Maimonides to list the belief in the prophecy of Moshe as a separate principle. Because of the unqualified importance of establishing, beyond question or doubt, the Divine origin of the Torah and thereby its eternal validity, great emphasis is put on the fact that the revelation of the Torah to Moshe was through the most direct "one-to-one" relationship with the Divine. Three Biblical verses establish this:

1. And the Lord spoke to Moshe face to face, as a man speaks to his friend . . . (Shemot 33:11).
2. With him I speak mouth to mouth, plainly and not in riddles, and he beholds the likeness of the Lord . . . (Bemidbar 12:8).
3. And there has not arisen a prophet since in Israel whom the Lord knew face to face (Devarim 34:10).

The revelation of the Torah on Mount Sinai was an event unparalleled in history. In the minds of those who witnessed that event there could be no question as to the source of Moshe's words, their Divine origin. Yet, the Lord chose to reinforce what they perceived, and we read, "And when the voice of the horn waxed louder and louder, Moshe spoke and God answered him by a voice" (Shemot 19:19). Here Rashi comments: "The Holy One Blessed Be He assisted him by giving him strength so that his voice might be powerful and so become audible." What is clearly alluded to here is the initiation of a partnership of sorts in the transmission of the Torah to Israel. We shall have more to say about this partnership later.

Moshe descends Mount Sinai bearing the second Tablets, and his skin radiates "beams of glory" visible to all Israel. From where did these beams come? How were they bestowed upon Moshe, and what did they symbolize?

The Prophet Habakkuk, in his symbolic portrait of the Almighty, saw beams radiating forth from His hand. We read:

> When God from Teman came, and the Holy One from Mount Paran Selah, His Glory covered the heavens and of His praise the earth was full; and His brightness was like the sunlight. *Beams streamed forth from His hand* unto them, and there was the hiding of His power.
>
> (Habakkuk 3:3, 4)

How interesting that the Supreme Being of the universe also radiates beams. Yet, even more significantly, these beams are termed *karnayim* by the prophet; they emanate from the "hand" of God.

It is our contention that the "beams of glory" with which Moshe was endowed — or *karne ha-hod,* as they are called in Hebrew — derived directly from God. Bestowed upon Moshe when he descended from Mount Sinai for the second time, they were meant to symbolize his unique power — his measure of Divine authority. It was this special authority that established the immutability of the Torah. Let us develop this idea somewhat more fully.

How did the second Sinai experience differ from the first?

In the first, Moshe was merely an observer; in the second, he was a participant. The first Tablets were hewn by the Almighty Himself; the

127

second, by Moshe. Rabbi Soloveitchik points out that, in the first experience, *Torah shebikhtav,* the Written Law, was revealed to him; in the second, *Torah sheb'al peh,* the Oral Law, was revealed as well.[51] Yet, still more took place on the mount the second time.

We have already learned that Moshe made two requests: to know God's ways and to know His essence. In response to the first, God revealed to Moshe the "Thirteen Attributes";[52] in response to the second, He told Moshe to stand on the rock. When God's glory would pass by, He would put Moshe in the cleft of the rock and cover him with His hand. God would then remove His hand and Moshe would see God's back.

Now, while it would be somewhat presumptuous for us to visualize what Moshe saw, and all the more so to describe it, to attempt to clarify what took place when God covered Moshe with His hand is quite another matter, for there is sufficient literature upon which to build a contention.

The symbolic hand of God that radiated beams covered Moshe, and God passed before him. Indeed, Moshe was "touched" by the Divine. But to what end? May the Torah be alluding to the fact that at that moment God bestowed upon Moshe the aforementioned Divine authority, and that it was effected through the transferrence of the "beams of glory" — or a measure thereof — from the hand of God to the face, the head, indeed, the mind of Moshe as he stood in the cleft of the rock? There is a Midrash that reinforces this contention:

You find sometimes: "And the Lord spoke unto Moshe," and "And

---

51. This point was made by J.B. Soloveitchik in a "yahrzeit lecture" in 1976.
52. Cf. Hayyim ben Atar, *Ohr ha-Hayyim,* and M. Malbim, *Ha-Torah V'ha-Mizvah,* Shemot 33:19.

the Lord said unto Moshe." So you also find: "And Moshe said unto the Lord," and "And Moshe spoke unto the Lord." It can be compared to a cave situated by the seashore, into which the sea once penetrated, and, having filled it, never departed, but was always flowing in and out of it. So it was that the Lord spoke to Moshe and Moshe said unto the Lord.

(Midrash Rabbah: Shemot 45:3)

There was a Divinely-induced reciprocity between God and Moshe, figuratively expressed by the Sages as the reciprocity between the cave and the sea. How poignant and significant is this analogy when we consider that the medium through which this reciprocity is established is water, the element so often likened to the Torah. The Midrash continues:

Whence did Moshe derive these beams of glory? The Sages said: From the cleft of the rock . . . R. Berakhiah the Priest said in the name of R. Shmuel: The Tablets were six handbreadths in length and six in breadth. Moshe grasped two handbreadths and the Presence another two, two handbreadths being left in the center, and it was from there that Moshe derived those beams of glory. R. Yehudah ben Nahman said in the name of R. Shimon ben Lakish: A little ink was left on the pen with which Moshe wrote, and when he passed this pen through the hair of his head, the beams appeared. . . .

(Midrash Rabbah: Shemot 47:11)

All three Midrashic explanations relate the "beams of glory" to the Torah, and symbolize the partnership between God and Moshe in the transmission of the Torah and the Oral Law to the children of Israel. The first sees this partnership in the measure of wisdom imparted by God to Moshe in the cleft of the rock. The second sees it in the participation of Moshe with God in the creation of the Tablets: they were hewn by Moshe and engraved by God. The third explanation focuses on the measure of participation, contrasting the participants. What was merely a "whisper" of the Divine — the "little ink" — was sufficient to make Moshe unique among the prophets.[53]

Let us now consider the veil with which Moshe covered his face when he was not studying or teaching the Torah. To prevent the symbolism of the "beams" from becoming commonplace out of sheer familiarity, Moshe employed the veil. Thus we read:

> And when Moshe had finished speaking with them, he put a veil on his face. But when Moshe went in before the Lord that he might speak with Him, he took the veil off, until he came out and spoke unto the children of Israel that which he was commanded. And the children of Israel saw the face of Moshe — that the skin of Moshe's face sent forth beams. And Moshe put the veil back upon his face, until he went in to speak with Him.
>
> (Shemot 34:33-35)

When Moshe was involved in the routine of daily living, his face was veiled. Only at designated times did he remove the veil — when he communed with the Lord to study the Torah and when he taught it to the people of Israel. Thus he brought attention to the "beams of glory" only when the symbolism was relevant. Each time Moshe unveiled his face before the people of Israel so that they looked upon the "beams of glory," the symbolism was reactivated in their minds, reminding them of the source of Moshe's teaching at the very time they were being taught, and thus reinforcing its declared immutability.[54]

---

53. Cf. Y. Arama, *op. cit.,* Devarim, *Sha'ar* 54.
54. Cf. Ibn Ezra, Ohr ha-Hayyim, and Y. Abravanel to Shemot 34:35.

When the time came for the reins of leadership to pass from Moshe to Yehoshua, it was of paramount importance to impress upon the elders as well as the masses of Israel that Yehoshua, too, had been endowed with an intellectual and prophetic ability. But it also had to be made clear that this endowment pertained primarily to the understanding and the teaching of *Torat Moshe* — the Torah that was given through the hand of Moshe:

> And the Lord said to Moshe: "Take Yehoshua, the son of Nun, a man in whom is spirit, and lay your hands upon him. Set him before Eleazer the Priest and before all the congregation and give him a charge in their sight. And you shall put of your glory upon him, that all the congregation of the children of Israel may hearken."
> (Bemidbar 27:18-20)

Yehoshua receives his measure of "glory" from God through Moshe, by the process of *semikhah:* the placing of the hands, the method first employed by God in transferring "glory" to Moshe. Thus Yehoshua assumes the role of supreme Torah authority. But when "glory" is transferred from one to another, it loses some of its "luster" — its weight of authority. Namely, what is rooted in the hand of the Lord fills the mind of Moshe. And what has been assimilated by Moshe is not fully transferred to Yehoshua. Thus we read in the *Sifre:*

> "And you shall put *of* your glory upon him" — but not *all* your glory. We thus learn: The face of Moshe was as the face of the sun and the face of Yehoshua was as the face of the moon.
> (Sifre: Bemidbar 27:20)

But still more is implied in the *Sifre.* Just as the moon is merely a reflection of the sun, for it lacks light of its own, so, too, Yehoshua was merely a reflection of Moshe. His appointment to leadership was primarily because he was Moshe's protege, and as such the most qualified person to teach the Torah to the people of Israel.[55]

Having clarified the significance of the "beams of glory," it is appropriate to mention still another point concerning Moshe's unique prophetic ability. Our Sages focus on two apparently contradictory verses in attempting to ascertain the uniqueness of Moshe:

1. And the Lord called to Moshe and spoke to him from the Tent of Meeting (VaYikra 1:1).
2. And when Moshe went into the Tent of Meeting to speak with Him, he would hear the voice addressing him from above the cover that was on top of the Ark of the Testimony, between the two keruvim. Thus He spoke to him (Bemidbar 7:89).

Did Moshe commune with the Lord at will, or was it necessary for him to wait to be summoned, as with the other prophets? Needless to say, the former is certainly a greater perfection than the latter. Most commentators posit that Moshe had to wait to be summoned by God to prophesy. The verse in VaYikra 1:1 sets the precedent for all Moshe's prophecies.

Maimonides, however, is of the opposite opinion, and writes the following:

All the prophets could not prophesy at will; not so with Moshe. Whenever he desired it, the holy spirit and the power of prophecy

---

55. Cf. Rabbenu B'haye, Bemidbar 27:20, and Yehoshua Pollak, *Binyan Yehoshua* to *Avot D'Rabbi Natan* 1:3.

rested upon him. There was no need for him to concentrate especially and prepare for it; he was always ready and prepared, like the ministering angels of the Lord. Therefore, he could prophesy at any time, as it is written, "Stand by, and let me hear what instructions the Lord gives about you."

(Mishneh Torah: Laws Concerning
Foundations of the Torah 7:6)

Abravanel agrees with the position of Maimonides, but derives it from a different source. He teaches that whenever Moshe wanted to commune with God he would enter the Tent of Meeting and immediately hear the Lord's voice. The perception was not dependent upon God's calling, but rather upon Moshe's will, as is indicated in Bemidbar 7:89. The situation in VaYikra 1:1 was the exception. The Tabernacle was being erected and the Glory of God was within. Under those circumstances, Moshe was not allowed to enter. Therefore, God called to Moshe from the Tent of Meeting.[56]

Lastly, we must point out that Moshe attained a level of prophecy above and beyond that for which he was prepared naturally. This was by virtue of the fact that he was involved with Israel. Yet, no other prophet in Israel was so privileged.[57] Now, while the level a prophet attains through his own preparedness stays with him forever, that which he attains due to other considerations is of a temporary nature. It may be removed by God if the circumstances for which it was bestowed change. As such, we can understand the words of our Sages, who, on the verse "Hurry down, for your people whom you brought out from the land of Egypt have acted basely" (Shemot 32:7),

---

56. Cf. Y. Abravanel, Bemidbar 7:89.
57. Cf. S. Linchitz, *Kli Yekar,* VaYikra 1:1.

comment: "This means, go down from your high position. I have given you distinction only for their sake" (Berakhot 32a). If Israel is to be destroyed, Moshe can no longer retain his special level of prophecy.[58]

---

58. *Ibid.*

Chapter 5

The Evidence of Strain

The rebellious behavior of the Israelites in the wilderness, in their long journey to Canaan, is not readily assessed. It would seem that the wonders they had witnessed in Egypt and on the Red Sea — and even the revelation of the Torah at Sinai — didn't suffice to cleanse them from the primitive ways of the Egyptians. From time to time, the Torah illustrates this point. And though the contention that this behavior was often initiated by the *erev rav,* the mixed multitude that had accompanied them from Egypt, is verifiable in the Torah text, it is still very much to their dishonor.[59] We will examine two such incidents of rebellious behavior. The Torah records:

> They marched from the mountain of the Lord a distance of three days. The Ark of the covenant of the Lord traveled in front of them on that three days' journey to seek out a resting place for them, and the Lord's cloud kept above them by day, as they moved on from camp. When the Ark was to set out, Moshe would say: "Advance, O Lord! May Your enemies be scattered and may Your foes flee before You!" And when it halted, he would say: "Return, O Lord, You who are Israel's myriads of thousands."
>
> (Bemidbar 10:33-36)

---

59. Cf. Y. Abravanel, Bemidbar 11:1, also Y. Arama, *op. cit., Sha'ar* 75.

What is the significance of the opening verse here? A most interesting discussion on the matter is found in the Talmud:

"When the Ark was to set out, Moshe would say . . ." For this section, the Holy One Blessed Be He provided signs above and below [it is preceded and followed by an inverted letter *nun*], to teach that this is not its place. Rabbi said: It is not at all on that account, but because it ranks as a separate book. . . . R. Shimon ben Gamliel said: This section is destined to be removed from here and written in its proper place. And why is it written here? In order to provide a break between the first account of punishment and the second. What is the second account? "And the people took to complaining" (Bemidbar 11:1). The first account? "They marched from the mountain of the Lord" (Bemidbar 10:33), which R. Hama ben Hanina expounded as meaning that they turned away from following the Lord.

(Shabbat 115b-116a)

According to Rashi, the "turning away" to which R. Hama ben Hanina referred was the demand that Moshe provide them with meat. This was their sin. An entirely different approach is taken by the Tosafists. The Israelites had been studying Torah for a full year, but when they left Sinai they refrained from study for three days. They literally marched themselves away from that which was represented by Sinai. The Tosafists illustrate the point quite graphically with an analogy: just as a child runs from school, so did they run from Sinai for three days. This act was, indeed, a grievous sin.

The second sin, which took place immediately afterwards, was twofold:

And the people took to complaining bitterly before the Lord. The

136

Lord heard and was incensed. A fire of the Lord broke out against them, ravaging the outskirts of the camp.

(Bemidbar 11:1)

The mixed multitude in their midst felt a gluttonous craving. And the Israelites, moreover, wept and said, "If only we had meat to eat! We remember the fish that we used to eat free in Egypt, the cucumbers, the melons . . . Now our gullets are shriveled. There is nothing at all, nothing but the manna to look to!"

(Bemidbar 11:4-6)

What is the difference between the first complaint, that led to the ravaging of the camp by the Lord, and the second? The first was an indication of their depressed state — they were unhappy with the present and their God-promised destiny for the future. The second was a betrayal of their lust for food. Both indicated that they had not yet outgrown their attachment to Egyptian culture and that they were not yet ready to be God's people. But while the first incident drew a ravaging fire from the Lord, with no response from Moshe, the second elicited some quite shocking and enigmatic words. Had Moshe at last reached the limit of his patience? The Torah records:

Moshe heard the people weeping, group after group, every person at the entrance of his tent. The Lord was very angry, and Moshe was distressed. And Moshe said to the Lord: "Why have You dealt ill with Your servant, and why have I not enjoyed Your favor, that You have laid the burden of all this people upon me? Did I conceive this people, did I bear them, that You should say to me, 'Carry them in your bosom as a nurse carries an infant,' to the land that You have promised to their fathers? Where am I to get meat to give all this people, when they whine before me and say, 'Give us meat to eat'? I cannot carry all this people by myself, for it is too much for me. If

You would deal thus with me, kill me, rather, I beg You, and let me see no more of my wretchedness."

(Bemidbar 11:10-15)

The disgraceful and thankless behavior of the people should have motivated Moshe to lash out at them in thunderous condemnation. How strange, then, that instead Moshe complains to God. We hear words that we would never have expected. An interesting comment is made here by R. Eliezer Ashkenazi. When Moshe heard the demand of the people for meat and witnessed God's anger, he tried to appease God with an apology for the people's behavior. The impropriety was not due to their failure, but rather to his limitations. Were he to have had assistants who would circulate among the people, pacify them, and win their approval, none of this would have happened. Focusing on Moshe's language, R. Ashkenazi contends that he compared the murmuring of the people to the cries of a child and himself to a nursing mother in order to emphasize that it was not ungratefulness that motivated the people's impropriety, but primitive-like fear. Such fear could only be assuaged by continuous "hand-holding" tactics, which would necessitate assistants.[60]

Focusing on the analogy to a "nursing mother," Joseph B. Soloveitchik makes an interesting point. What is the role of a nursing mother? She must carry her child in her bosom, always watching . . . always anticipating. Her own needs become secondary to those of the child. Indeed, there is a fusion of the two identities. Now, as demanding and as self-sacrificing as this role may be, the mother is usually quite willing to assume it, for it is vital to the proper nurturing of the child.

---

60. Cf. E. Ashkenazi, *Ma'ase Hashem:* Ma'ase Mizrayim, Vol. II, Chapter 19.

Moshe felt that his responsibilities toward the nation had changed; he had become a "nursing father," and this new role disturbed him. Although he knew that it was necessary in those formative years of Jewish nationhood, he had difficulty accepting the fact that, in his new role, family obligations and concerns would have to be relegated to second place. The fact that he had to a great extent relinquished his duties as husband and father to become the "father of Israel" was a difficult pill for him to swallow, for he was human, with human needs and human desires. Naturally, then, he resisted this new role which the vicissitudes of life had thrust upon him. He was truly taken aback and distressed. These thoughts motivated his complaint which, in consideration of his humanness, was certainly understandable.[61]

In response to Moshe's request for help in his new leadership role, the Lord appointed seventy elders. They would be chosen by Moshe and sanctioned by God: "Then the Lord came down in a cloud and spoke to him; He drew upon the spirit that was upon him and put it upon the seventy elders" (Bemidbar 11:25). The seventy elders, men of great wisdom and Divine authority, were those who knew the people best, who could commiserate with them in their problems, and yet who could see things objectively. They were the men who had been appointed as judges over the people back in Egypt, and were trusted implicitly by them. Here again we have an example of Moshe's great leadership ability.[62]

The number seventy is rich in symbolism. As Rabbenu B'haye points out, the Heavenly Court is composed of seventy angels and the Sanhedrin in Jerusalem was composed of seventy scholars. With

---

61. The point was made by J.B. Soloveitchik at a lecture given at Yeshiva University on Purim 1974.
62. Cf. Rashi, Bemidbar 11:16.

Moshe presiding over them, the elders totaled seventy-one, corresponding to the Heavenly Court: one angel for each of the seventy nations of the world, and the Lord presiding over them, totaling seventy-one. This number also symbolizes the number of souls that had gone down to Egypt; with Jacob, they were seventy-one. Lastly, says Rabbenu B'haye, the Sanhedrin totaled seventy; with the president, they were seventy-one.[63]

More, says Rabbenu B'haye, just as the power of the seventy angels in the Heavenly Court derived from God, so the power of prophecy of the seventy elders derived from Moshe's power. And just as God's power was in no way diminished by this phenomenon, neither was that of Moshe.[64] Interestingly, while the power to prophesy could have come to the elders directly from God, it did not. Instead, it came from Moshe. Had this spirit come to the elders directly from God, it might have swelled their egos and tempted them to challenge Moshe's authority over them.

Parenthetically, it is interesting to note that throughout the Bible the spirit of God that enables man to prophesy rests *upon* him, not *within* him. Shimshon Raphael Hirsch on Bemidbar 11:17 enlightens us:

> The term used for imparting the spirit of prophecy is sharply different from those used to refer to every other kind of spirit which God grants. . . . All such gifts of spirit from God were an increase in the spiritual capacity of the recipients. What resulted from such spiritual gifts and inspiration did not exceed the normal measure of human capacity. It remained human words and human acts borne and elevated by special gifts and inspiration from God. But the spirit of

---

63. Cf. Rabbenu B'haye, Bemidbar 11:16.
64. Cf. *Sifre,* Bemidbar 11:17.

prophecy does not proceed from within; it comes onto a person . . .
it is something Divine of which a man becomes the bearer . . .
What he says and what he does is God's word and God's doing, and
the man is merely His conveyer and His agent.

That prophecy comes from "without" rather than from "within" is a
fundamental principle of Judaism. A person may be perfectly qualified
and totally prepared to prophesy, constitutionally and otherwise, and
yet not do so. Only God initiates the encounter.[65]

Moshe's request is to be granted. Seventy elders will be appointed as
aides and judges. But first the people are to be punished for their
rebellious act:

> And say to the people: Be ready for tomorrow and you shall eat meat,
> for you have kept whining before the Lord, saying, "If only we had
> meat to eat!" You shall eat not one day, not two, not even five days or
> twenty, but a whole month, until it comes out of your nostrils and
> becomes loathsome to you.
>
> (Bemidbar 11:18-20)

The punishment befits the crime! In fact, it is probably more
embarrassing and degrading than anything else God might have done.
Here again, Moshe's response is enigmatic:

> The people who are with me number six hundred thousand men; yet
> You say, "I will give them enough meat to eat for a whole month."
> Could enough flocks and herds be slaughtered to suffice them? Or
> could all the fish of the sea be gathered for them to suffice them?
>
> (Bemidbar 11:21, 22)

---

65. We have already noted that Moshe was the singular exception to this principle.

Is Moshe questioning God's omnipotence? That is hardly imaginable. Nevertheless, God's response is crushing: "Is there a limit to the Lord's power?" (Bemidbar 11:23). What is the significance of Moshe's words and God's response? Has Moshe finally given up on his people? Has God lost patience with him?

Rashi relates an interesting difference of opinion between R. Akiva and R. Shimon. The *Sifre* teaches that this is one of the four Biblical passages where these two Sages differ in their interpretation. R. Akiva understands Moshe's words literally: How could the flocks they had brought suffice for them to eat meat for a full month? R. Shimon feels that one must read between the lines to ascertain Moshe's intention. Moshe feared that God was about to destroy the people. They would be fed and then annihilated. Would this be proper? asked Moshe. R. Shimon feels that Moshe was concerned with God's honor. How would it appear to the world if God were to perform a great miracle for Israel, only to destroy them immediately thereafter? How reminiscent of Moshe's argument after the sin of the golden calf!

"If I don't feed them now," said the Lord, "it will be said that God's power is limited. Would that be pleasing to you? Let them and a hundred like them perish, but let not the Lord's power appear to be limited!"

How interesting that R. Akiva had no qualms of conscience in taking the literal interpretation of the Biblical text, even though it is a clear condemnation of Moshe. What's more, says R. Akiva, the only reason Moshe was not punished at this time was because he had not taken this position publicly.[66]

An interesting and most insightful approach to these verses is taken

---

66. Cf. Rashi and *Sifre,* Bemidbar 11:22.

by Rabbenu B'haye in Bemidbar 11:21. He writes:

> Far be it from our minds to think that Moshe doubted the Creator's power. He said: "The people who are with me number six hundred thousand men. They are of little faith, not at all worthy of a miracle. Yet, by natural means, there would simply not be enough meat for them." It was Moshe's opinion that their request should not be granted for they were only testing God. . . . But the Holy One Blessed Be He answered him: "Is the Lord's power so limited that He cannot grant their request and provide them with sufficient food naturally? You shall see whether My words can be fulfilled. Gather unto Me seventy of the elders of Israel, for I will take of the spirit that is upon you and put it upon the seventy, and it will suffice. . . . Just as the spirit that is upon you is one, yet it will suffice for seventy elders, so am I able to provide meat for this vast nation — not through a miracle at all, but through natural means."

True, the Israelites are not worthy of a miracle, says God to Moshe, but I can provide sufficient food for them in a natural way, despite their great number.

Quite in tune with Rabbenu B'haye's thinking we then read that the Lord caused the spirit of Moshe to pass over to the elders, as He had promised, and they prophesied. Almost immediately thereafter we read: "And a wind went forth from the Lord and brought quail from the sea" (Bemidbar 11:31). They came from the sea, their natural habitat. There was no need for a miracle.

After the spirit of prophecy passed from Moshe to the elders, the Torah records an interesting incident. Two men, Eldad and Medad, prophesied in the camp. They were not among the seventy elders, yet the spirit of prophecy seemed to have rested upon them. They prophesied that Moshe would die and Yehoshua would lead the

Israelites into the Promised Land.[67] The Torah records:

> And Yehoshua, the son of Nun, Moshe's attendant from his youth,
> spoke up and said, "My lord Moshe, restrain them." But Moshe said
> to him, "Are you wrought up on my account? Would that all the
> Lord's people were prophets, that the Lord put His spirit upon them."
> (Bemidbar 11:28, 29)

The fact that Eldad and Medad not only prophesied the death of
Moshe, but also made known their prophecy during his lifetime,
elicited a severe condemnation from Yehoshua. With it, an interesting
point comes to the surface. It was Yehoshua who condemned them,
though he was glorified by their words; it was Moshe who condoned
their behavior, though his dreams and hopes were shattered by their
prophecy. So another facet of Moshe's character is revealed to us in the
Torah: his great respect for the word of God and his love of truth,
despite the fact that it carried great personal disappointment.

It is of interest that immediately after the episode of Eldad and
Medad the Torah records another impropriety, this time emanating
from none other than Miriam and Aharon, and directed against Moshe.
Here, however, it seems to be merely a matter of idle gossip:

> Miriam and Aharon spoke against Moshe because of the Cushite
> woman he had married, for he had indeed married a Cushite woman.

---

67. Cf. Sanhedrin 17a. This is the position of R. Shimon, but there are two other
views. R. Hanin, on the authority of R. Eliezer, said that they prophesied
concerning the quails, and R. Nahman said that they prophesied concerning the
battle of Gog U'Magog.

They said: "Has the Lord spoken only through Moshe? Has He not spoken through us as well?"

(Bemidbar 12:1)

We have already discovered from the *Chronicles of Moshe* that Moshe had married an Ethiopian woman and separated from her before going to Midian. Some commentators contend that it was this woman of whom Miriam and Aharon spoke. Others contend that they meant Zipporah, and that the appellation "Cushite woman" was complimentary, meaning "a dark, beautiful woman."[68] But what was the problem?

The Midrash teaches that from the time the Torah was revealed to him at Sinai Moshe had withdrawn from sexual activity. Evidently, Miriam was aware of this condition; she noticed that Zipporah no longer adorned herself with the customary jewelry. Curious, Miriam approached her and asked. When she was told that Moshe no longer cared about those things, she drew the appropriate conclusions. Somewhat disturbed with the situation, she repeated it to her brother Aharon, and they spoke against Moshe.[69]

Miriam had condemned Moshe for denying his wife her conjugal rights. On what basis had she done so? There is no indication from either the Biblical text or the commentary that Zipporah was perturbed over the matter. Had Miriam spoken against Moshe out of jealousy, over his having attained the highest degree of prophecy? Or was it her

---

68. Cf. Rashi, Bemidbar 12:1.
69. Cf. *Yalkut Shimoni* I, 4337. Another view brought here is that Miriam was with Zipporah when the youth came by to report that Eldad and Medad were prophesying in the camp. When Zipporah heard him, she remarked: "Woe unto the wives of these men." Then Miriam knew and told her brother, and they spoke against Moshe.

brother's uneasiness about his new role as a "nursing father" that motivated her to enlist the help of Aharon to bring Moshe back to his family?[70]

Before we resolve this question, let us digress for a moment and consider Moshe's action: his separation from his wife. Does Judaism condemn or in any way discourage normal sexual relations between a husband and wife? Were the prophets charged with celibacy?

The only event where the Torah relates sexuality to prophecy is the revelation of the Law at Sinai. The entire nation was addressed by Moshe with the words: "Be ready for the third day: do not go near a woman" (Shemot 19:15). When the masses of the people of Israel were to be elevated to prophecy, they were told to desist from sexual relations, a fundamental aspect of their humanness and that which they had in common with the animal world. Thus, they transformed themselves temporarily into spiritual beings. This was not to imply that sexual relations was wrong or degrading, but rather to emphasize its place in man's life — that it should be of secondary importance to him, his primary focus being on the spiritual and intellectual. Needless to say, this charge was limited to the three-day period. After the revelation, God speaks to Moshe, saying: "Go, say to them, 'Return to your tents.' But you remain here with Me, and I will give you the whole instruction — the laws and the norms — which you shall impart to them to observe in the land that I am giving them to possess" (Devarim 5:27, 28).

According to Malbim, the quasi-angelic state that the Israelites had attained at Sinai by rising above their material element was only temporary. It was to cease; they were then to return to their human

---

70. Cf. M. Malbim, *op. cit.,* Bemidbar 12:1, 2.

condition and engage in normal human activities. Moshe, on the other hand, would retain this condition for the rest of his life.[71] The Talmud explains:

> And he (Moshe) separated from his wife . . . reasoning: if the Israelites with whom the Presence spoke only on one occasion and He appointed them a time thereof, yet the Torah said, "Be ready for the third day: do not go near a woman," I, with whom the Presence speaks at all times and does not appoint me a definite time, how much more so. And how do we know that the Holy One Blessed Be He gave His approval? Because it is written, "Go, say to them: 'Return to your tents,' " which is followed by: "But you remain here with Me."
>
> (Shabbat 87a)

Again, we must point out and emphasize that Moshe was unique. He was in a continuous state of preparedness; the spirit of prophecy rested upon him at all times. Yaakov Zvi Mecklenberg explains that with all of the other prophets, when the spirit of prophecy came upon them, their bodies became weak and their limbs began to tremble, until their souls were able to separate from their bodies and relieve the trauma. Only then did they prophesy. Not so with Moshe. Even when he was awake and conscious, his material element was so pure that it in no way affected his ability to prophesy. Indeed, Moshe was able to attain the height of prophecy while his soul rested within his body.[72]

Unbeknownst to Miriam and Aharon, Moshe was in a state of perpetual readiness to receive the Divine word. Had they been aware of this, they might have understood the necessity for his separation from

---

71. *Ibid.,* Devarim 5:27.
72. Cf. Y.Z. Mecklenberg, *op. cit.,* Bemidbar 12:7.

his wife Zipporah.[73] Their enlightenment came from the Almighty Himself, quickly and most dramatically: "Suddenly the Lord called to Moshe, Aharon, and Miriam: 'Come out, you three, to the Tent of Meeting.' So the three of them went out" (Bemidbar 12:4).

Why the sudden command? And why is Moshe included?

The sudden revelation demonstrated quite clearly to Miriam and Aharon that they were completely unprepared for the Divine word, while Moshe was ready and able. Thus the message rang out loud and clear: Moshe is unique. He cannot be treated, or expected to conduct himself, like the rest of the nation of Israel.

Considering that Miriam's impropriety was merely an error in judgment, why was she punished by the Lord? Even after Moshe pleads for her, she is ostracized — put outside the camp for seven days. Perhaps it was because she was audacious in daring to question Moshe's behavior. We must remember that, although he was her brother, he was the Lord's appointed leader of Israel. As such, her impropriety may have been considered a sin against the Almighty as well. One must also consider the effect her going unpunished would have had on the masses.[74]

Moshe pleads in her behalf. There was not a single reprimand from the innocent party. This befits the description the Torah gives here of Moshe: "Now, the man Moshe was very humble, more so than any other man on earth" (Bemidbar 12:3).

---

73. Cf. Y. Arama, *op. cit., Sha'ar* 76.
74. *Ibid.* It is noteworthy that, here again, the punishment complemented the sin. *Zara'at* has been traditionally associated with evil talk, a sin man commits against his fellow man. In truth, however, it is also a sin against God, for the person affected by this plague is being touched by God's displeasure. Cf. S.R. Hirsch, Bemidbar 12:10.

The people make ready to enter the land of Canaan and they send out spies to inspect the land, study its terrain and people, and report to them on the conditions. Much to their disappointment, the spies return with a bad report. The people panic: "And they said to one another, 'Let us head back for Egypt.' Then Moshe and Aharon fell on their faces before all the assembled congregation of Israel" (Bemidbar 14:4, 5).

Once more, the people display their lack of confidence in both God and Moshe. Once more we wonder how, after all those miracles, they still lacked the faith and trust to continue their journey to the Promised Land . . . to enter it and to conquer. It would certainly seem to us that this generation was not at all ready to inherit the land promised to Avraham, Yizhak, and Yaakov. In point of fact, they would never be ready. So they were walled into the wilderness, where they would remain for the rest of their lives. Thus we read the depressing pronouncement of the Lord:

> In this very wilderness shall your carcasses drop. All of you who were recorded in your various lists from the age of twenty years up, you who mutter against Me, not one shall enter the land in which I swore to settle you — save Calev, son of Yefuneh, and Yehoshua, son of Nun. Your children, who you said would be carried off — these will I allow to enter; they shall know the land that you have rejected. . . . You shall bear your punishment for forty years, corresponding to the number of days — forty days — that you scouted the land: a year for each day. Thus you shall know what it means to thwart Me.
>
> As for the men whom Moshe had sent to scout the land, those who came back and caused the whole community to mutter against him by spreading rumors about the land, those who spread such rumors about the land died of plague by the will of the Lord. Of those men who had gone to scout the land, only Yehoshua, son of Nun, and Calev, son of Yefuneh, survived.
>
> (Bemidbar 14:29-38)

It was a bitter pill, indeed, for the Israelites to swallow. But for Moshe it was particularly distressing and disappointing, for he had anticipated leading Israel into the land, building the Temple, and bringing on the Messianic Era.

Moshe had appealed to the Lord for forgiveness of the people, and the Lord had forgiven them as He had done with the sin of the golden calf. Yet, it would seem that some punishment had to be borne by them. Or perhaps it was not a punishment at all, but rather a practical decision on the Lord's part. This nation, with its slave mentality, who had been groomed in Egypt, the center of idolatry, could never relinquish its ties to that culture. At the slightest provocation, the people lost their faith and resorted to the ways of Egypt. Only the new generation, groomed by Moshe and untainted by the abominations of Egypt, was capable of tackling the awesome task of conquest.

Let us backtrack a bit and study Moshe's argument to the Lord in behalf of Israel. It has a familiar ring:

> But Moshe said to the Lord, "When the Egyptians, from whose midst You brought up this people in Your might, hear the news, they will tell it to the inhabitants of the land. Now they have heard that You, O Lord, are in the midst of this people; that You, O Lord, appear in plain sight, when Your cloud rests over them and when You go before them in a pillar of fire by night. If then You slay this people to a man, the nations who have heard Your fame will say, 'It must be because the Lord was powerless to bring that people into the land which He had promised them on oath that He slaughtered them in the wilderness.' "
>
> (Bemidbar 14:13-16)

The argument is quite similar to the one Moshe put forth after the sin of the golden calf. As we did there, we must now ask, "What difference can it possibly make to God what the Egyptians think or say?" An insightful answer is given by Yaakov Zvi Mecklenberg.

We are well aware, says R. Mecklenberg, that God's purpose in performing all the wonders in Egypt was not to torture the Egyptians, but to bring them to recognize His existence and His limitless providential concern. In fact, many of them did come to this. The Torah speaks of them as "those who feared God" (Shemot 9:20). Even Pharaoh remarked, "God is the righteous one, and I and my people are in the wrong" (Shemot 9:27). If God were to destroy the Israelite nation, all the wonders He had performed in Egypt would have been for naught, for the Egyptians would no longer believe the things they had learned from experience about God's omnipotence and His concern. Quite the contrary: they would now say that His power functions against the Egyptian gods, but He is powerless against the gods of Canaan. Such an assumption would be a desecration of His name. The nation of Israel, therefore, had to be preserved.[75]

God works in much broader themes than measure for measure punishment. The greater goal — indeed, the ultimate goal — is the reeducation of mankind. The good that had been accomplished in Egypt in that regard could be nullified in one fell swoop.

It is a logical and most noble argument. As a fitting conclusion, Moshe invokes the attributes God had revealed to him at Sinai as a final plea for the forgiveness of the people of Israel:

> Therefore, I pray, let my Lord's forbearance be great, as You have declared, saying, "The Lord, slow to anger and abounding in kindness, forgiving iniquity and transgression; yet not remitting all

---

75. Cf. Y.Z. Mecklenberg, *op. cit.*, Bemidbar 14:13.

punishment, but remembering the iniquity of the fathers for the sake of the children, upon the third and fourth generations." Pardon, please, the iniquity of this people, according to Your great kindness, as You have forgiven this people ever since Egypt.

(Bemidbar 14:17-19)

It is important to note that the Divine attribute "slow to anger" has special significance here. The Talmud explains:

When Moshe ascended on high, he found the Holy One Blessed Be He sitting and writing (of Himself), "slow to anger." Said Moshe to Him, "Sovereign of the universe! Slow to anger with the righteous?" He replied, "Even with the wicked." He (Moshe) urged, "Let the wicked perish!" "See what you desire," was His answer.

When Israel sinned, He said to him, "Did you not urge Me, 'Let Your attribute *slow to anger* apply to the righteous only?' " "Sovereign of the universe!" said he, "but did You not assure me, even to the wicked?"

(Sanhedrin 111a)

The Almighty is slow to anger with both the righteous and the wicked. This is a basic tenet of Judaism. The sin of the golden calf was Israel's first sin as a nation; they had not lost their status as a righteous people, and they were forgiven as such. Here, however, they had become seasoned sinners. Were it not for the fact that God is slow to anger with the wicked as well, they would never have been forgiven.[76]

---

76. God's long suffering of the wicked is to give them the opportunity to repent. Although such forbearance with the wicked is conversely tolerant of the wicked, there is no other option if man is to remain free. Cf. Eliezer Berkovits, *Faith After the Holocaust* (New York, 1973), pp. 101-107.

It must be made clear that Moshe had not asked for absolution, but rather an easing of the punishment. This request was granted. They were not destroyed *en masse,* but allowed to die natural deaths, one by one, during the forty years in the wilderness.[77]

The Korah Rebellion

Although we have discussed several incidents of rebelliousness among the people, these were primarily manifestations of restlessness and fear of the unknown that were expressed in complaint against God and Moshe. In all these incidents, Moshe came to the aid of his people; he was their spokesman; he was their advocate; he was their protector. Indeed, the people relied on him throughout their journey in the vast, unsearched wilderness. Deep in their hearts, they trusted him and loved him. They knew that as long as they were under his leadership no harm would come to them. Even after the sin of the golden calf, only a few of the people were executed. Bearing this in mind, we can state with reasonable assuredness that, under those conditions, the people would never have tolerated a rebellion against Moshe.[78]

But the air changed. When the people came to the wilderness of Paran, many of them were ravaged by the Divine fire at Tav'erah, and many others were executed at Kivrot ha-Ta'avah. When they were punished and told that they would die in the wilderness, never to reach their destination, the people became terribly embittered. They began to feel that Moshe's guidance had led them astray, and the stage was set for disaster.[79]

---

77. Cf. Rabbenu B'haye, Bemidbar 14:17.
78. Cf. Ramban, Bemidbar 16:1.
79. *Ibid.*

Korah, son of Yizhar, of the tribe of Levi, along with Datan, Aviram, and two hundred fifty men, took this opportunity to initiate a rebellion that purported inequity in the leadership of Moshe and Aharon. As with most politicians, it was not the welfare of the people that Korah sought, but rather the enhancement of his own power and political goals.

Rabbenu B'haye explains that the rebellion was motivated by Korah's envy and an error in judgment that no harm would come to him. The rebels argued that all the decisions and all the appointments to leadership made by Moshe were for personal reasons. It was the all too familiar argument of nepotism which, at a different time, under different circumstances, and with a different leader might well have been plausible. It was not the case here, for the appointments made by Moshe were Divine appointments, from Moshe on down. As we already know, Moshe himself had to be persuaded by the Lord to assume the leadership of Israel. Likewise, it was the Lord who had sanctified the firstborn. Regrettably, they had forfeited that privilege when they sinned with the golden calf, and their place was taken by the Tribe of Levi.[80]

It has already been noted by some commentators that the rebellion was not really against the leadership per se but against the appointments to the priesthood. It was not Moshe whom they wished to impeach, but Aharon and his sons. The complaint against Moshe was that he had appointed them. We must also keep in mind that Korah, himself a Levite, felt that he deserved to be the High Priest. The point is implied in Moshe's response to Korah's complaint:

---

80. Rabbenu B'haye, *op. cit.*

Then he spoke to Korah and all his company, saying, "Come morning, the Lord will make known who is His and who is holy. . . . He will grant access to the one He has chosen. . . . You have gone too far, sons of Levi." Moshe said further to Korah, "Hear me, sons of Levi. Is it not enough for you that the God of Israel has set you apart from the community of Israel, by giving you access to Him to perform the duties of the Lord's Tabernacle, and to minister to the community and serve them? Thus He has advanced you and all your fellow Levites with you; yet, you seek the priesthood too. Truly it is against the Lord that you and all your company have banded together. For who is Aharon that you should rail against him?"

(Bemidbar 16:5-11)

If it is true that all the people are holy as you suggest, says Moshe, let us put it to the test. Take censers with incense and let all of you offer the *ketoret,* the incense, to the Lord, as Aharon and his sons do. The Lord Himself will designate who are the holy ones. Moshe then turned to Datan and Aviram. He approached them separately because they had challenged him personally, concerning his right to leadership. He attempted to persuade them to end the rebellion and thus avoid disaster, but to no avail.[81]

Now let us recognize that the rebellion did far more than question Moshe's judgment and propriety in his appointments to the priesthood, and his right to the leadership of Israel. It undermined Moshe's integrity and the authenticity of his prophecy; it could easily have resulted in an outright rejection of the Divinity of the Torah by the entire nation. As such, the punishment of the rebels had to be most severe.[82] But even more was needed. The Torah records:

---

81. Cf. S.R. Hirsch, Bemidbar 17:29, 30.
82. Cf. Rabbenu B'haye, Bemidbar 16:29.

And Moshe said, "By this you shall know that it was the Lord who sent me to do all these things, that they are not of my own devising. If these men die as all men do, if their lot be the common fate of all mankind, it was not the Lord who sent me. But if the Lord brings about something unheard of, so that the ground opens its mouth wide and swallows them up, with all that belongs to them, and they go down alive into the grave, you shall know that these men have spurned the Lord."

(Bemidbar 16:28-30)

If the rebels had died natural deaths, the punishment would not have simultaneously served to establish the authenticity of Moshe's mission. For the mission was initiated through prophecy, that process through which God communicates with man, demonstrating that He is above and beyond the laws of nature. By referring to God with the name Lord, the Tetragrammaton, a name which symbolizes God's ability to introduce a completely new future not dependent upon the past, Moshe implied that the punishment would be through a means that was beyond the laws of nature. The rationale would be as follows: since the rebels had questioned the Divine quality of Moshe's mission, God would afflict them with a supernatural punishment, thus demonstrating that at times it is His will to act upon the world in a supernatural way. By being done at Moshe's request, this punishment would also demonstrate that God communicated with Moshe through the supernatural medium of prophecy. The penalty would authenticate Moshe's mission.[83]

What was the punishment? The Torah records the following:

Scarcely had he finished speaking all these words when the ground

---

83. Cf. S.R. Hirsch, Bemidbar 17:29, 30.

under them burst asunder, and the earth opened its mouth and swallowed them up with their households — all Korah's people and all their possessions. They went down alive into the grave with all that belonged to them. The earth closed over them, and they vanished from the midst of the congregation. . . . And a fire went forth from the Lord and consumed the two hundred and fifty men offering the incense.

(Bemidbar 16:31-33, 35)

Quite an astonishing phenomenon. But what made this a miracle? After all, earthquakes are common occurrences. According to Nahmanides, the miracle lay in the fact that the earth returned to its former condition after it had swallowed up the rebels. This is never the case with an earthquake.[84] According to Rabbenu B'haye, the fact that both heaven and earth participated in the punishment made it both a miracle and a true manifestation of measure for measure retribution. The rebels, who spoke against the Torah, symbolically and literally the foundation of heaven and earth, were punished by heaven and earth. The fire came down from heaven, ravaging the two hundred fifty men, and the earth swallowed up Korah's people.[85]

---

84. Cf. Ramban, Bemidbar 16:30.
85. Cf. Rabbenu B'haye, *op. cit.*

Chapter 6

Shall Even the Mighty Fall?

We have discussed several incidents of strife that occurred in the wilderness during the forty-year journey to Canaan. They presented some difficulties, but for the most part we were able to resolve them. The most enigmatic event of that period, however, the "Waters of Strife" incident — Mei Merivah — is not so readily resolved. The difficulty lies not in the murmuring of the people; we are quite used to such murmuring by now. It is the behavior of Moshe that is perplexing. He defied the word of God, and this is incomprehensible. The Torah records the following:

> The Israelites arrived — the entire nation — at the wilderness of Sin on the first new moon, and the people stayed at Kadesh. *Miriam died there and was buried there.* The community was without water, and they joined against Moshe and Aharon. The people quarreled with Moshe, saying, *"If only we had perished when our brothers perished before the Lord!* Why have you brought the Lord's congregation into this wilderness for us and our beasts to die there? Why did you make us leave Egypt, to bring us to this wretched place, a place with no grain or figs or pomegranates? There is not even water to drink."

> Moshe and Aharon came away from the congregation to the entrance of the Tent of Meeting, and fell on their faces. The Presence of the Lord appeared to them, and the Lord spoke to Moshe, saying,

"You and your brother Aharon *take the rod* and assemble the community, and before their very eyes *order the rock* to yield its water. Thus you shall provide water for them from the rock, and provide drink for the congregation and their beasts."

Moshe took the rod from before the Lord, as He had commanded him. Moshe and Aharon assembled the congregation before the rock, and [Moshe] said to them, "Listen, you rebels, shall we get water for you out of this rock?" And Moshe raised his hand and *struck the rock twice* with his rod. Out came copious amounts of water, and the community and their beasts drank.

But the Lord said to Moshe and Aharon, "Because you did not trust Me enough to affirm My sanctity in the sight of the Israelites, therefore you shall not lead this congregation into the land that I have given them." Those are the waters of Merivah — meaning that the Israelites quarreled with the Lord — through which He affirmed His sanctity.

(Bemidbar 20:1-13)

Many questions arise in our minds when we read this story. We shall focus on four points of interest:

1) What is the significance of recording Miriam's death here?
2) What did the people mean when they said, "If only we had perished when our brothers perished before the Lord"?
3) Why was Moshe told by the Lord to take the rod with him if he was only to speak to the rock?
4) What precisely was the sin of Moshe and the significance of the punishment meted out to him by the Lord?

Our Sages give two reasons why Miriam's demise was recorded at this point. The first adjoins the event to the preceding material, the law of the red heifer; the second adjoins it to the incident at Merivah. The Talmud teaches, in the name of R. Ami: "Why is the death of Miriam adjoined to the section on the red heifer? To teach you that, just as the red heifer brings atonement, so does the death of the righteous" (Moed Katan 28a).

For what sin was the death of Miriam an atonement? The sin of the golden calf. But how are the two related? In a brief but concise analogy, the Midrash clarifies the connection:

> Said R. Ibo: It can be compared to the child of a maidservant who soiled the palace of the king. Said the king, "Let his mother come and clean up the waste." So said the Holy One Blessed Be He, "Let the cow come and atone for the deed of the calf."
>
> (Bemidbar Rabbah 19:4)

In a sense, just as Moshe was the "nursing father" of the Jewish people, Miriam was their "nursing mother." Her death atoned for the horrendous sin of the golden calf, for it occurred at the end of the forty years of wandering through the wilderness, when all of the old generation had died out. Figuratively speaking, Miriam was, indeed, the "red heifer" of Israel.

As for the second reason why Miriam's death is recorded here, the Talmud teaches that Israel had three great leaders in their journey through the wilderness: Moshe, Aharon, and Miriam. The Israelites were given three precious gifts through these leaders: the pillar of cloud that protected them during the day, the manna that sustained them, and the well that supplied them with water, the last of which was through the merit of Miriam. When Miriam died, the well dried up, and the incident at Merivah came about.

Whether the words of our Sages are to be understood literally —

God gave Israel a miraculously self-replenishing well that quenched their thirst through the forty years — or symbolically — He gave them the Torah, which is frequently likened to fresh living waters — the implication is quite clear. Despite her one impropriety, Miriam was an exemplary human being, and all Israel was nourished by her life.[86]

Our first question having been answered, we proceed to the second. The words "If only we had perished when our brothers perished before the Lord" clearly refer to the older generation, who had left Egypt and had by now died out. What was their nobility? They had died before the Lord — by His decree and in His service. As Shimshon Raphael Hirsch explains: "They had all died before God. God's care had not forsaken them, right to their last breath. Their deaths went the way of the natural mortality of human beings, without being brought about by any dreadful calamity — but we are to perish by thirst," said the people (Bemidbar 20:3).[87]

Thirdly, we asked why Moshe was told to take the rod with him, when he was instructed to speak to the rock rather than smite it. Let us begin by pointing out that the rod had very special significance, which was symbolic rather than functional: Moshe carried the rod to represent an idea rather than to perform miracles. It had no innate power. What then was its symbolism?

Abravanel contends that it represented royal authority, and indicated to the people that Moshe had spoken and acted in the name of God.[88] Shimshon Raphael Hirsch adds: "The staff in the hands of Moshe designated him as being sent by God. A movement with the staff — a waving, a blow with it before an announced event took place —

---

86. Cf. Ta'anit 9a.
87. Cf. Y. Abravanel, Bemidbar 20; also Y. Arama, *op. cit., Sha'ar* 80.
88. *Ibid.*

proclaimed that event to be the result of a momentary direct intervening act of God" (Bemidbar 20:8). Others claim that it was Aharon's rod that Moshe had taken this time, the rod which had blossomed and had borne fruit at the time of the Korah rebellion to symbolize the chosenness of Aharon and his sons. At the time, Moshe had placed Aharon's rod in the Ark before the Lord in the Tent of Meeting. It would serve now as a sign to the rebels, which is why Moshe called out to them, "Listen, you rebels."[89] Just as it had demonstrated Aharon's chosenness — for God had acted upon it and caused it to blossom — so, too, would the rod represent Moshe's chosenness. This would be a lesson of crucial importance to the new generation.

Our fourth question will necessitate greater and more developed elucidation. In any study of Moshe, the appropriateness of his behavior at the "Waters of Strife" incident is of major concern. Let us first take note, however, that Masah U'Merivah and Mei Merivah were one and the same. The first time the Israelites had come there and thirsted for water, Moshe was instructed to smite the rock; the second time, to speak to it. It would be quite logical for us to assume, then, that the two incidents are thematically related. We must also take note of the fact that what happened at Masah U'Merivah was experienced by the generation of the Exodus, while what happened at Mei Merivah was experienced by their children in the fortieth year of their wandering, as they were about to enter Canaan.[90]

Although there are many different approaches as to what happened at Mei Merivah and why it happened, we shall focus on the interpretation of Yizhak Arama, whose explanation is quite extraordinary.

89. Cf. Hizkiah ben Manoah, *Sefer Hizkuni,* Bemidbar 20:8.
90. Cf. Avraham Ibn Ezra, Bemidbar 20:1.

It is not at all strange, says R. Arama, that the Israelites, having lived in Egypt for more than two centuries, were affected to some extent by their culture, which denied the existence of a Heavenly Court and God's concern for man. Moshe was always suspect in the eyes of the Israelites. Perhaps his great wisdom or cleverness, rather than God's intervention, had brought the Egyptians to their knees. So they watched him very closely — studying his moves, words, and ways for evidence that would confirm their suspicions. At Masah U'Merivah, things came to a head. How was it possible, they thought, that the omnipotent and omniscient God would have directed them to a place where there was no water? If Moshe really spoke for the Lord, they should have lacked for nothing. This doubt initiated a confrontation.

It was of the utmost importance that the people witness a miracle with the very substance through which their suspicions were aroused. This would finally uproot their erroneous thinking and end their presumptuousness. And so it was.[91]

At Mei Merivah, however, the older generation had died out, and a new generation had arisen, who were not witness to the events at Masah U'Merivah. They were in the wilderness of Sin. Miriam had died and the well that had sustained them had now run dry. In the same place, facing the same predicament, once again suspicion reared its ugly head against Moshe and Aharon. The people demanded water.[92]

Human nature does not change; it carries through from one generation to the next as if implanted in the genes. Again a miracle had to be performed to establish Moshe's Divine authority. But for this generation it had to be something more wondrous than before. It was necessary to demonstrate that God's power is not limited to one kind of

---

91. Y. Arama, *op. cit., Sha'ar* 80.
92. *Ibid.*

miracle, to be repeated whenever necessary. That would be a desecration of God's name.

Of equal consideration was the desired effect upon the people. We must bear in mind that this generation had been raised with miracles. What would be shown to them had to be of greater impact than what was shown to their parents in order for them to be truly moved and sufficiently impressed. In order to finally put to rest the suspicion about Moshe — that his cunning and power alone had taken them out of Egypt and was responsible for their destiny — it was crucial that neither he nor any of the elders be physically involved in the execution of this miracle. Indeed, it had to be made perfectly clear that Moshe was merely God's messenger.[93]

The following would have been accomplished had Moshe complied with God's command and spoken to the rock.

Firstly, it would have been a sanctification of God's name of the highest proportions, as well as an authentication of the mode of prophecy. By demonstrating their unqualified commitment to God's word, to the point where they would be willing to present themselves before the entire congregation of Israel and announce the performance of an astonishing act, knowing full well the embarrassing — indeed detrimental — consequences if it failed, Moshe and Aharon would have established the truth of prophecy for all time. This would have been of unparalleled importance, for it would have inspired the new generation to a greater commitment to God and to Torah.[94]

Secondly, to demonstrate that not only the animate, but the inanimate in nature as well, is responsible to God, would have truly

---

93. *Ibid.*
94. *Ibid.*

magnified God's power; it would have taught a lesson heretofore unknown to the masses of Israel.[95]

Lastly, had Moshe and Aharon abstained from any physical involvement with this miracle, they might have had a profound and truly lasting effect upon the people. While striking the rock would have supported the old suspicion of Moshe that had now manifested itself in the new generation — that this was not a miracle at all but just another example of Moshe's adeptness at magic — speaking to the rock would have neutralized such a suspicion. It would have convinced the people that the Almighty Himself had produced this phenomenon — that it was a miracle. Consequently, it would have stilled the daily complaints of the people and had a significant effect on their behavior.[96]

Alas, what could have been is not what was, and hindsight serves no purpose for us here but to explain the seriousness of Moshe's blunder — for it was not done maliciously. Perhaps he faltered because he was preoccupied with the vexing problems of the people; they had so tired him that he had misinterpreted the Divine word.

Let us emphasize that our intent is certainly not to judge Moshe, only to comprehend his actions. We will note, however, that this incident is one more example of a point made in the Torah from time to time about our forefathers: they were human beings, not angels. As such, they were subject to human emotions and human foibles. But this is not meant to be taken in a derogatory sense; it is not to demean their accomplishments, but to highlight them.

The punishment of Moshe and Aharon regarding this incident is mentioned three times in the Torah:

---

95. *Ibid.*
96. *Ibid.*

But the Lord said to Moshe and Aharon, "Because you did not trust
Me enough to affirm My sanctity in the sight of the Israelites,
therefore *you shall not lead this congregation into the land* that I have
given them."

(Bemidbar 20:12)

For you both were unfaithful to Me among the Israelites at the waters
of Merivat-kadesh, in the wilderness of Sin, by failing to uphold My
sanctity among the Israelites. You may view the land from a distance,
but *you shall not enter it* — the land that I am giving to the Israelite
people.

(Devarim 32:51, 52)

. . . Ascend these heights of Avarim and view the land that I have
given to the Israelite people. When you have seen it, *you too shall be
gathered to your kin,* just as your brother Aharon was. For in the
wilderness of Sin, when the community was contentious, you
disobeyed My command to uphold My sanctity in their sight by
means of the water.

(Bemidbar 27:12-14)

If the sin was threefold, it follows that the punishment would be
threefold as well, says Yizhak Arama:

The first sin related to their status in Israel. Moshe and Aharon were
prophets and leaders; they faltered in establishing their unqualified
faith, which could have set a profound example for the people.
Consequently, they were removed from leadership at the point of its
ultimate reward — entry into the land. As the text indicates, new
leaders would be appointed to take the nation into Canaan.[97]

The second sin related to the honor of the Almighty. By
demonstrating that even inanimate matter submits to God's will, they

---

97. *Ibid.*

would have established His unlimited rule in the universe, a manifestation of His ultimate perfection. By refusing to allow Moshe and Aharon to enter the land, God withheld from them their ultimate perfection — the fulfillment of those mitzvot that are dependent upon the land.[98]

The third sin was related to God's omnipotence. By speaking to the rock, they would have demonstrated His limitless power — He performs the supernatural with no necessity whatsoever for man's participation. By smiting the rock, Moshe frustrated, so to speak, the intent of the Almighty. People might have interpreted this act of Moshe as a statement that man is God's partner, that he must always be the medium through whom God's will is fulfilled. Such a statement would be heresy; because of it, Moshe was punished with premature death. This is clear from the juxtaposition of God's decree that Moshe was to die with the sin of disobedience. The point is spelled out in the Talmud, in the name of R. Shimon ben Eleazer: "Moshe and Aharon, too, died through their sin,[99] for it is said, 'Because you did not believe in Me . . .' (Bemidbar 20:12). Hence, had you believed in Me, your time had not yet come to depart from the world."[100]

From the interpretation of Yizhak Arama, therefore, it is clear that the punishment fit the crime. It was an example of measure for measure retribution. And although it seems like too severe a punishment for so great a man as Moshe, we must bear in mind that the greater the man

---

98. *Ibid.*
99. Shabbat 55b. The text here is quoted by Y. Arama in the name of the *Sifre* as follows: "R. Shimon ben Eleazer said: Moshe and Aaron died by excision, for it is said, 'Because you did not sanctify Me, etc.' — their time had not yet come to depart from the world."
100. Cf. Y. Arama, *op. cit.*

the greater his influence, the greater his responsibility, and the greater is his punishment if he falters.

There is another approach to the sin of Moshe that bears note. It is the interpretation of Shimshon Raphael Hirsch on Bemidbar 20:8. He writes:

> They (the people) are to be made to see that it was not Moshe, but the Lord, who led them to this place . . . that it was not just their stormy agitation that necessitated and caused the intervention of the Lord, but rather that the required water was already provided by the Lord at the place to which *He* had directed them, and that it merely required a word from Moshe and Aharon to the rock which would suffice to produce the water which the Lord had placed ready for them. This manner of obtaining water from the rock would have convinced the people of the deep wrong they had done in accusing Moshe and Aharon of leading them to this waterless place against the will of the Lord. However, the waters gushing forth only as a result of the blow of the rod could still leave room for the assumption that their having been led into the wilderness of Sin was originally a willful arbitrary act of Moshe and Aharon, and only subsequently the justified revolt and the pressing need brought about the merciful miracle of the Lord. It would have taught the people that under the guidance of the Lord one can dismiss all worries from one's mind and, even without the miracle-causing rod of Moshe, can be confident at all times of the right help coming at the right time.

A blow with the rod indicated not only that a miracle had just been performed, but that in response to a need that had now arisen a miracle had just been conceived. This implied that no provision for water had been made in advance. But this was precisely what the event was *not* meant to imply. By speaking to the rock, Moshe would have demonstrated that the water had already been there, that the Lord had brought the Israelites to a place where only He knew there was water. It would have taught them the lesson of providence, that God is continuously concerned with mankind, and the people of Israel in particular.

In conclusion, the "Waters of Strife" incident was a lost opportunity to have a profound influence on the thinking, the behavior, and the destiny of the nation of Israel. It was a frustration of God's plan. Inadvertent as the sin may have been, it could not go unpunished.

Chapter 7

The Death of Moshe

Throughout our studies of Moshe, we have never come across even a single instance when he requested a favor for himself. Even when he asked to know God's ways and His essence, it was only to enable him to be a better leader of Israel. Moshe neglected his responsibilities to his wife and children — by Divine command, to be sure — in order to properly fulfill his mission. Only at the end of his life did Moshe break this rule and request something for himself:

> I pleaded with the Lord at that time, saying, "O Lord God, You who let Your servant see the first works of Your greatness, and Your mighty hand, You whose powerful deeds no god in heaven or on earth can equal! Let me, I pray, cross over and see the good land on the other side of the Jordan, that good hill country and the Lebanon." But the Lord was wrathful with me on your account and would not listen to me. The Lord said to me, "Enough! Never speak to Me of this matter again."
>
> (Devarim 3:23-26)

Moshe's request was sharply and unalterably denied. Why? What was the meaning and significance of the request? What motivated him to ask, having already been told that he would not enter the land?

The Talmud records the following lesson:

170

R. Simla'i expounded: Why did Moshe our teacher yearn to enter the
land of Israel? Did he want to eat of its fruit or satisfy himself from its
bounty? But thus spoke Moshe: "Many precepts were commanded to
Israel which can only be fulfilled in the land of Israel. I wish to enter
the land so that I may fulfill them all."

(Sotah 14a)

Moshe, the giver of the Law, aspired to its total fulfillment. Since
many of the commandments either pertained directly to the land or
applied only in the land, he would have to be there in order to observe
them. This was the sole reason for his persistence.

Yizhak Abravanel elaborates: Moshe knew that the reigns of
leadership had to pass to Yehoshua, his attendant, who had the stamina
to fight and conquer, to triumph over kings, and to lead the nation into
the Promised Land. Moshe was not plagued by a desire to do so
himself. He wanted only to enter the land and live there like the rest of
Israel, to worship and to observe the commandments.[101] Perhaps he
yearned to experience the sacredness of the land firsthand, to see it with
his eyes . . . to feel it under his feet . . . to touch it. But this was not to
be Moshe's destiny. He would never return to his former condition.
There is no turning back in life.

Moshe had another request. He wanted to die as his brother Aharon
had died, peacefully and nobly. This request was to be granted. And so
we read: "You shall die on the mountain you are about to ascend, and
shall be gathered unto your people as Aharon your brother died in
Mount Hor and was gathered unto his people" (Devarim 32:50). How
beautifully the *Sifre* depicts the scene:

---

101. Cf. Y. Abravanel, Devarim 3, p. 23.

"As Aharon your brother died: the death you envied." How do we know that Moshe envied the death of Aharon? Because God told him, "Take Aharon and Eleazar his son. Remove his sacred garments and put them on Eleazar." God said to Aharon: "Enter the cave." He entered. "Rise up onto the bed." He rose up. "Stretch out your limbs." He did so. "Close your mouth." He did. At that moment, Moshe said, "Happy is the man who dies in such a way."

In order to better comprehend the way in which the Almighty took Moshe from the world of the living, we must first focus on the text. The Torah records:

Moshe went up from the steppes of Moav to Mount Nevo, to the summit of Pisgah, opposite Yericho, and the Lord showed him the whole land: Gilad as far as Dan; all Naftali; the land of Efrayim and Menashe; the whole land of Yehudah as far as the western sea; the Negev and the Plain — the valley of Yericho, the city of palm trees — as far as Zoar. And the Lord said to him: "This is the land which I swore to Avraham, Yizhak, and Yaakov: 'I will give it to your offspring.' I have let you see it with your own eyes, but you shall not cross there."

So Moshe the servant of the Lord died there, in the land of Moav, at the command of the Lord. He buried him in the valley of the land of Moav, near Bet-Peor; and no one knows his burial place to this day.

Moshe was a hundred and twenty years old when he died; his eyes were undimmed and his vigor unabated. And the Israelites bewailed Moshe in the steppes of Moav for thirty days.

The wailing period in mourning for Moshe came to an end. Now, Yehoshua, son of Nun, was filled with the spirit of wisdom, because Moshe had laid his hands upon him, and the Israelites heeded him, doing as the Lord had commanded Moshe.

Never again did there arise in Israel a prophet like Moshe, whom the

Lord singled out face to face, for the various signs and portents that the Lord sent him to display in the land of Egypt, against Pharaoh and all his courtiers and his whole country, and for all the great might and awesome power that Moshe displayed before all Israel.

(Devarim 34:1-12)

Several questions arise from these concluding verses of the Torah:

1) Was Moshe's experience on Mount Nevo merely visual?
2) Why was it that Moshe, the chief of prophets, had to die like an ordinary human being while prophets like Eliyahu and Hanokh, clearly of lesser stature, were taken to heaven alive?
3) What was the significance of Moshe's burial?

When Moshe was on Mount Nevo, he was shown the panorama of Jewish history. As the *Sifre* points out, there are key words in each of the Biblical verses that allude to historical events. True, he would not participate in these events, but he would witness them, much like standing in the wings of the theater — more than a mere bystander, yet not a performer. Somewhat like a documentary, God would cause the events of Jewish history to pass before Moshe's eyes. It would be a highly sensuous, emotional, and intellectual experience — this despite the fact that he was merely a witness. In truth, a great deal more was granted to Moshe than to the patriarchs. In God's own words: "To the patriarchs I swore an oath, but I showed it to you to see with your own eyes" (Devarim 34:4).[102]

---

102. Cf. *Sifre,* Devarim 34:1-3.

A fine delineation of what was shown to Moshe is found in the commentary of Yizhak Abravanel:

Since Moshe was not to cross over the Jordan River to see the land, the land would figuratively cross over to him. This is alluded to in the other name given to Mount Nevo: *Har ha-Avarim,* literally, "the mount of crossings." Perhaps, in a limited sense, it would fulfill his request. He saw the whole country; its cities and towns were before his eyes. Yet he saw far more than just the land; he saw the development of Jewish history. He saw the joy and the sadness, the formation of the state and its destruction.[103] In the words of Abravanel:

> God showed him the events that would take place in this land in the future: the conquest, the succession of kings, the division of the kingdom, and the destruction of the Jewish state. Each event was seen in its proper place and time. . . . It was as if he were witnessing them as they were happening.[104]

Our first question answered, we proceed to the second. We begin by posing a moot philosophical question: Is the human condition — body and soul united in life — the ultimate fulfillment of God's design for man, or is there a further stage to be fulfilled? If the former is true, we can understand why Eliyahu and Hanokh were taken to heaven alive, and our question concerning Moshe is legitimate. If the latter is true, as we shall assume here, it needs further elaboration. Let us turn again to Abravanel.

King Solomon said: "And the dust returns to the ground as it was and

---

103. Y. Abravanel, Devarim 34, p. 340.
104. *Ibid.,* p. 341.

the soul returns to God who bestowed it" (Kohelet 12:7). He reveals in this statement that the purpose of man and his ultimate destiny is fulfilled at death, when the two elements of which he is composed separate absolutely from each other, so that not a shred of one remains in the other. For it is impossible for any person, be he the most perfect of men, to live eternally, never to experience death. . . .[105]

When the body, bereft of spirit, returns to the earth from which it was taken, and the soul, bereft of matter, returns to its Creator, God's ultimate plan for man has been fulfilled.[106] But total and absolute separation of body and soul does not occur with the onset of death. It is a gradual process. For in life, body and soul are closely involved with each other, so much so that they are virtually inseparable. When death occurs, the magnetic-like attraction is so strong that they cling to each other. Though they separate, the body retains some impurities from its union with the soul. This is what the Sages mean when they refer to the impure spirits that exist in the dead. Since this is the condition of most people in death, the Torah decreed a state of impurity upon the dead body for a period of twelve months, during which time the soul ascends to heaven and descends to the earth, until finally all shreds of the soul have left the body and it can return to the earth whence it was taken.[107]

There are some people, however, who have for the most part succeeded in bringing their material element under the control of their intellect. The bond and blend of body and soul are not the same with them as with others. With death and the separation of body and soul, the body is not sufficiently strong to retain threads of the soul. Yet

---

105. Devarim 34, p. 344.
106. *Ibid.,* pp. 344-345.
107. *Ibid.,* p. 345.

neither is the soul sufficiently strong to separate itself entirely from the body. It retains some impurities from the body, which rise with it to heaven, to its special place, where it remains until it separates from those impurities, totally and absolutely, and returns to its Creator, from which it came. This was the case with Eliyahu. He rose, body and soul, heavenward, to the sphere of fire, where his entire body was consumed, after which his soul returned to God, who had given it.[108]

Lastly, there are some individuals, few in number, indeed, whose lives have been so perfect that when death comes body and soul are able immediately to separate from each other, totally and absolutely, each returning to its origin. The bodies of these rare individuals never enter a state of impurity. Our Sages teach that Moshe our teacher was indeed a man of such nobility; the Torah itself proclaimed him to be so. With the onset of death, his body and soul separated immediately from one another and returned to their origins. As such, the Almighty Himself engaged in his burial.[109]

In answer to our second question, the way in which Moshe departed from this world was a manifestation of the highest level of sanctity, and hence most fitting for the chief of prophets.

Our last question concerned the significance of Moshe's burial.

It is clear from the writings of our Sages that Moshe was not only unique in life; he was unique in death as well. As the Torah testifies, until the very last moment of his life, "his eyes were undimmed and his vigor unabated." And when his body returned to the earth from which it was taken, say the Sages, it did so extraordinarily. Again we refer to the explanation of Abravanel:

When Moshe died, the Almighty did not allow his body to suffer

---

108. *Ibid.*
109. *Ibid.*

the humiliation of slow decay. At the moment of death, Moshe's bodily parts separated from one another and quickly returned to the natural elements. What was left was the purest form of dust — no flesh, sinews, or bones. This clear, fresh dust was immediately absorbed into the earth, leaving no trace behind.[110]

In life, Moshe was Israel's staunchest advocate; in death, he was their greatest loss. It was a loss felt throughout Jewish history, and is destined to be felt for all time. How beautifully the Midrash depicts the feeling:

> When Moshe's soul had fulfilled its alloted time on earth, the Holy One Blessed Be He commenced and said: "Who will take My part henceforth against evil men? Who will take Israel's part before Me when I am angry with them? Who will stand up for Me when My children are engaged in battle? Who will plead for mercy for them when they sin against Me?"
>
> At that moment, the angel Matatron came forth, fell upon his face, and said: "Master of the universe! In life he was Yours, and in death he is Yours."
>
> Said the Holy One Blessed Be He: "I will draw you an analogy. To what can this be compared? To a king who had a son who so angered him that he threatened every day to kill him. Only the child's mother was able to save him. When she died, the king wept bitterly. His servants said to him, 'Our master and king, why do you weep?' He said to them, 'I do not weep only for my wife, but for my son as well. For many were the times that I was so angry with him that I wanted to kill him, but she saved him from me.' " So did the Holy One Blessed Be He say to Matatron, "Not only for Moshe am I saddened and do I weep, but for all Israel as well."
>
> (Midrash on the Death of Moshe:
> Ozar Midrashim, p. 376)

---

110. *Ibid.*, p. 349.

ᵀₕₑEternal Heritage

A lucid translation of classic and contemporary
traditional sources on the Torah

THE ETERNAL HERITAGE presents to the English reader
access to early and later commentators such as:

- Ramban
- Radak
- Ohr HaChayyim
- R. Bachya
- Kli Yekar
- Chatham Sofer
- Chafetz Chaim
- Maharal
- Vilna Gaon

- R. Simcha Bunem of Pshischa
- R. Levi Yitzchak of Berdichev
- R. Shlomo Kluger
- Divrei Shaul
- R. Yitzchak Zev Soloveichik
- R. Meir Yechiel of Ostrovtsa
- Pardes Yosef
- Chiddushei HaRim
- Meshech Chochmah

THE ETERNAL HERITAGE gives access to the English-speaking public to many Torah commentaries that until now were available only in Hebrew.

By Avraham M. Goldstein

DREAMS

By RABBI SHMUEL BOTEACH

DREAMS. Where do they originate? How significant is their content? How are they to be interpreted?

While many believe that the importance of dreams was neglected until the advent of psychology, the truth is that Jewish sources spoke of dreams and their meaning centuries ago. The Torah itself — in the stories of Yosef and Pharaoh — emphasizes that dreams are a matter to be dealt with seriously.

DREAMS makes the world of sleep, as seen through the eyes of the Torah, awaken. The pronouncements of our Sages on this topic are brought to life in a cohesive, fluid text. The reader will come to understand how Judaism sees the nature and role of dreams, and the importance of their content.

DREAMS captures the Torah view of dreams in a style that will please layman and scholar alike.

Soon to be published